Central Conference of American Rabbis

Birkon Artzi

BLESSINGS AND MEDITATIONS
FOR TRAVELERS TO ISRAEL

Rabbi Serge A. Lippe, editor

With a Foreword by Rabbi Rick Jacobs

and an Introduction by Bruce Feiler

Library of Congress Cataloging-in-Publication Data

Birkon Artzi : blessings and meditations for travelers to Israel / Serge A. Lippe, editor; with a foreword by Rick Jacobs and an introduction by Bruce Feiler.
   p. cm.
   Includes bibliographical references and index.
   ISBN 978-0-88123-189-2 (pbk. : alk. paper)
   1. Judaism--Prayers and devotions. 2. Travelers--Israel. 3. Reform
  Judaism. I. Lippe, Serge A., 1964- II. Central Conference of American Rabbis.

  BM665.B54 2012
  296.7'2--dc23

2012020508.

CCAR Press

Cover Painting: Menashe Kadishman, *Haheder Bnof* (Flock of Sheep in Landscape), 1981, acrylic on canvas. Used by permission of the artist. **Photo Credit:** Kadishman, Menashe (1932–) Untitled, 1981. Acrylic on canvas, 74 x 80 in. (188 x 203.2 cm). Gift of Henry Welt, 1986-153. Photo by Johen Parnell. The Jewish Museum, New York, NY, U.S.A. Used by permission of The Jewish Museum, New York/Art Resource, NY.

16 15 14 13 12 6 5 4 3 2 1
CCAR Press, 355 Lexington Avenue, New York, NY 10017
(212) 972–3636, ccarpress@ccarnet.org
www.ccarpress.org

Acknowledgments

Reform Jews have been traveling to the Land of Israel, *Eretz Yisrael*, since long before the establishment of the modern state, *M'dinat Yisrael*. From Rabbi Judah Leon Magnes, the founder and first chancellor of the Hebrew University, to Rabbis Stephen S. Wise and Abba Hillel Silver, to Louis Brandeis and Henrietta Szold, Reform Jews have been journeyers and participants in the unfolding of Zionism and champions of the modern State of Israel.

Since 1958 thousands of Reform Jewish teenagers have traveled to Israel under the auspices of the North American Federation of Temple Youth (NFTY). In 1963 Hebrew Union College–Jewish Institute of Religion established its Jerusalem campus and since 1970 has sent its first-year rabbinical, cantorial, and education students there for their first year of studies. In 1973 the World Union for Progressive Judaism (WUPJ) moved its international headquarters to Jerusalem, and in 1976 the WUPJ became the first international Jewish religious organization to affiliate with the World Zionist Organization (WZO).

That same year the CCAR affirmed in its "Centenary Perspective" that "We are bound to...the newly reborn State of Israel by innumerable religious and ethnic ties....We have both a stake and a responsibility in building the State of Israel, assuring its security and defining its Jewish character."

Today, with some thirty synagogues members of the Israel Movement for Progressive Judaism, two kibbutzim (Yahel and Lotan) in the Aravah, a moshav (Har Halutz) in the Galilee, the renowned Leo Baeck School in Haifa, the Israel Religious Action Center, and over seventy Israelis ordained as Progressive rabbis, Reform Jews visiting from around the world can also connect with the vital and native branch of Reform Judaism in our people's homeland.

This *birkon** seeks to create spiritual opportunities and responses for the thousands of Reform Jews who journey each and every year to visit, study in, and support the State of Israel. We journey through Israel not as mere travelers or tourists, but as visiting family, seeking to pause and acknowledge place and moment, and to create connection and fashion memory. In doing so, we are fulfilling a mitzvah. As the 1997 CCAR "Miami Platform" urges, "To deepen awareness of Israel and strengthen Jewish identity, we call upon all Reform Jews, adults and youths, to study in, and make regular visits to, Israel."

We recognize that there is a spiritual uniqueness and qualitative difference in traveling to *M'dinat Yisrael* in *Eretz Yisrael*. As Jews whose origins link us to many lands and nations, we affirm our commonality in this particular journey to our ancestral homeland in the modern State of Israel.

I am deeply grateful to Rabbi Hara Person, my colleague, friend, and former housemate in Israel, and to the CCAR Press especially Rabbi Steven A. Fox, Deborah Smilow, Debra Hirsch Corman, Rabbi Jillian Cameron, Ortal Bensky, and Rabbinic intern Yael Rooks-Rapport, for encouraging my concept and patiently guiding it to completion.

My acknowledgment and thanks to the members of the CCAR Israel *Birkon* Task Force for guiding, contributing to, and improving this work: Rabbi Heidi Cohen, Rabbi Karen Fox, Rabbi Micah Greenstein, Rabbi Rick Jacobs, Rabbi Paul Kipnes, Rabbi Janet Liss, Rabbi Garry A. Loeb, Rabbi David E. Stern,

---

*What exactly is a *birkon*? In Yiddish we call it a *bencher* (a book of benedictions). Rather than a siddur, composed for the fixed prayers of the synagogue, a *birkon* is a blessings booklet, one might even say a portable "pocket edition," of those prayers that are recited for travel, at special locations or events, or at meals.

Rabbi Mark Strauss-Cohn, Student Rabbi Josh Weinberg, and Rabbi Michael Weinberg. I would also like to thank the members of the Worship and Practice Committee who also reviewed the manuscript and made helpful suggestions, including the Chair, Rabbi Elaine Zecher, and Rabbis David Adelson, Nicole Greninger, Rosie Haim, Larry Hoffman, Tamar Malino, Joel Mosbacher, Rex Perlmeter, Beth Schwartz, Joel Sisenwine, and Rabbi/Cantor Alison Wissot.

The notion of a *birkon* was deeply influenced first and foremost by the work of my teacher Rabbi Lawrence Hoffman, who established the modern genre in his *Israel—A Spiritual Travel Guide: A Companion for the Modern Jewish Pilgrim*. This effort in no small way stands upon the shoulders of his work and vision. Also deeply affecting and influential has been the poet Danny Siegel's collection *Before Our Very Eyes: Readings for a Journey through Israel*. Finally, Jeremy Gimbel's *Birkon Mikdash M'at: NFTY's Bencher* demonstrated that this format could fill an unmet need for the Reform Movement.

Many thanks to the members of the Brooklyn Heights Synagogue, who have encouraged this project in no small part (especially our member John Levy, who travels to Israel regularly and asked if one of "these" didn't already exist—now it does!), and especially the students and faculty of our current and previous ninth grade religious school classes who have journeyed each May on our annual Israel class trip.

Finally, my most important thanks to my wife, Deborah Speyer, who took her first journey to Israel with me, and to our children, Michael, Alex, and Risa, who will be making their own first *n'siot* soon!

N'siot tovot – good travels!

Rabbi Serge A. Lippe

Foreword: My Heart Is in the East

by Rabbi Rick Jacobs

I fell in love with Israel during my junior year of college, which I spent studying at the Hebrew University in Jerusalem. What is the source of my passion for Israel? Yehuda Halevi best expressed my commitment when he wrote: "My heart is in the East."

I love the extraordinary and complex mosaic that is contemporary Israel: the secular, the settlers, the peaceniks, the Reform, the Orthodox, the Bedouins, the new immigrants, the *chalutzim*, the Arab-Israelis, the left, the right, and the center. They are all part of my Israel.

To me, Jewish life cannot be imagined without Israel at its core. Occasional disagreements with Israeli policies are a necessary part of serious engagement with our Jewish state. But our love for Israel is not dependent on who is prime minister or on what issues are before the Knesset or the chief rabbinate.

Visiting Israel is one way that we can become involved with and supportive of Israel. When we travel to Israel, visit its sites, meet its people, eat its food, and walk its streets, we begin to form a living relationship with Israel that goes way beyond the headlines and the sound bites.

Aleinu – "it is up to all of us" to foster a deep love for and engagement with Israel. We need Israel and Israel needs us.

Israel is surely a bundle of issues and challenges. But it is also our dynamic, complex, and inspiring Jewish homeland. Israel is an inspiring source of Jewish creativity and identity.

I want everyone to have the opportunity to travel to Israel

and see the land that I love. I want to show them all of the hard parts but still I know they will fall in love with this place of miracles and courage. They will see the gorgeous faces of the Ethiopian children who marched across African deserts to reach the land of their prayers. They will marvel listening to Russian immigrants playing Bach concertos on the Ben Yehuda Mall. They will be moved by the dynamism of our Reform congregations in Tel Aviv and Haifa and Jerusalem and throughout the country. They will be amazed by the Reform kibbutzim in the Aravah. They will see the miracles that remain hidden to those who only know Israel from afar.

At 4 p.m. on Friday, May 14th, 1948, a very diverse group of Jewish leaders signed on to the Declaration of Independence. The 37 signators included communists, socialists, revisionists, rabbis, atheists, kibbutznikim, urbane city dwellers, Ashkenazim, Mizrachim, rich and poor.

It was an unlikely and very diverse group of Zionists bound together by a common vision that our people could one day live as a free people secure in our land. That same vision can unite us today as well. That is the vision that informs my deep and abiding commitment to and love for *M'dinat Yisrael*.

As the leader of the largest Movement in Jewish life, I work every single day to build up the ranks of those who share my Zionist passion. And I call upon everyone in the pro-Israel community to join me. Traveling to Israel is one piece of this critical work.

This booklet that you hold in your hands is your guide to uncovering the miracles and the magic of Israel. The words of these readings, ancient and modern, will help Israel find a place in your heart. And when Israel gets into our hearts, then we will never stop doing our part to help create an Israel that is secure, religiously free, guided by justice, and dwelling in peace.

Our hope is not lost—
The hope of two thousand years:
To be a free people in our land,
The land of Zion and Jerusalem.

Kein y'hi ratzon.

Excerpts on Israel from the CCAR Platforms

From the 1937 "Columbus Platform"

In the rehabilitation of Palestine, the land hallowed by memories and hopes, we behold the promise of renewed life for many of our brethren. We affirm the obligation of all Jewry to aid in its upbuilding as a Jewish homeland by endeavoring to make it not only a haven of refuge for the oppressed but also a center of Jewish culture and spiritual life.

From the 1976 "Centenary Perspective"

We are bound to…the newly reborn State of Israel by innumerable religious and ethnic ties.…We have both a stake and a responsibility in building the State of Israel, assuring its security, and defining its Jewish character.

From the 1997 "Miami Platform"

To deepen awareness of Israel and strengthen Jewish identity, we call upon all Reform Jews, adults and youths, to study in, and make regular visits to, Israel.…

The achievements of modern Zionism in the creation of the State of Israel, in reviving the Hebrew language, in absorbing millions of immigrants, in transforming desolate wastes into blooming forests and fields, in generating a thriving new economy and society, are an unparalleled triumph of the Jewish spirit.

We stand firm in our love of Zion. We resolve to work for the day when waves of Jewish pride and confidence will infuse every Jewish heart, in fulfillment of the promise: *When God restores the fortunes of Zion we shall be like dreamers. Our mouths will fill with laughter and our tongues with songs of joy. Then shall they say among the nations: God has done great things for them.*

Contents

Introduction

by Bruce Feiler

When I was in my early 30s, I decided I wanted to reread the Bible. I hadn't read it since I was child growing up as a Reform Jew in Savannah, Georgia, which meant I hadn't really read it. So I took my Bar Mitzvah Bible off my shelf, put it by my bed, where it sat, untouched, for two years, gathering dust and making me feel even guiltier. Then I went to visit an old friend who had made *aliyah* in Israel. On my first day in Jerusalem, a friend took me to the Promenade overlooking the city. "There," he said, pointing south, "is a controversial neighborhood. And there," he continued, pointing north to the golden dome in the heart of the Old City, "is the rock where Abraham went to sacrifice Isaac."

His comment hit me like a bolt of Cecil B. DeMille lightning. It never occurred to me those stories—so timeless, so larger than life—might have happened in places you could actually visit, touch, and feel. Instantly I had an idea. What if I retraced the Bible through the lands where it took place, read the stories along the way, and tried to make some connection to the places, the people, and the stories of my past?

Walking the Bible: A Journey by Land Through the Five Books of Moses was published several years later, and launched me on a fifteen-year course that included two more books, *Abraham* and *Where God Was Born*, a television series on PBS, and countless more visits to this spot. I can say with awe and appreciation, having now read Rabbi Serge Lippe's beautifully edited volume of blessings and meditations for travelers to Israel, that I wish I could have carried this invaluable book with me in my backpack, hip pocket, or (were I making such a trip today), e-reader.

It is full of surprising moments, perfectly turned phrases, and well-chosen words for reflection or worship. Few pilgrims who visit these lands in the future will want to go without it.

On nearly every page of this elegant book, which is helpfully arranged as if the reader is on a visit, there are words to stop you in your tracks and deepen your connection to a place. I love the opening of a poem by Amir Gilboa, which the editors recommend reading before retiring on a first night in Israel: "This whole land belongs to me sleeping and awake I see / one long electric flash of dream making." Who can fail to harken back to a fleeing Jacob laying his head on a rock? The same heart-stopping idea is contained in this ode to Jerusalem itself: "One does not travel to Jerusalem, one returns / One ascends the road taken by generations."

I have never met a Jew who did not a feel a complicated stir of emotions on visiting Israel, and the one piece of advice I always give travelers today is to step off the well-trod paths and try to have an encounter with the land. This book is designed to enhance and deepen that experience. "I am the kind of person who receives feeling through their feet, not through words or slogans," says Amos Klein in a meditation on walking. And Prime Minister Yitzhak Rabin, in an excerpt from his final remarks, captures the emotion of traversing these storied steps. In Israel, "there is no path that is without pain."

There is also no path without meaning, and that's what makes us keep coming back. "There are stars up above," says Hannah Senesh, "The stars that light up the darkest night / these are the stars that guide us." These stars are our past—both our collective history and our personal search for connection. Sometimes the best way to see them is to step out of our comfort zone and look up at the sky.

I have long felt about the Bible that its most alluring part is the incomplete spaces in between the words. There is not a story in the text that a good editor today would not send back and ask, "Wait! I want to know more!" But it is precisely those spaces that invite the traveler in. I can think of few better companions for how to elevate those moments than to take this book on that path with you. Come, as Abraham Joshua Heschel says in the pages, be stunned. Once you have done so, you will always return.

Bruce Feiler is the best-selling author of the international sensation *Walking the Bible*, along with its follow-ups, *Where God Was Born and Abraham*, as well as seven other books. He is also the writer/presenter of the PBS series *Walking the Bible*. He lives in Brooklyn, with his wife and twin daughters. For more information, please visit www.brucefeiler.com.

1 PRAYERS BEFORE LEAVING FOR ISRAEL

At a Congregational Service

יְיָ יִשְׁמָר־צֵאתְךָ וּבוֹאֶךָ מֵעַתָּה וְעַד־עוֹלָם.

Adonai yishmor tzeit'cha uvo-echa mei-atah v'ad olam.

May the Eternal One guard your coming and your going
from this time forth and forever.

(Psalm 121:8)

Meditation for a Group

May God who called our ancestors Abraham and Sarah to journey into the unknown, and watched over them and blessed
them, protect us too and bless our journey.

May Your Presence support us as we set out, may Your spirit
be with us on the way, and may You lead us back to our homes
in peace.

We entrust our loved ones to Your care. You are with them,
as with us, and we shall not fear.

As for ourselves, may Your Presence be our companion, so
that blessing comes to us, and to everyone that we meet.

בָּרוּךְ אַתָּה, יְיָ, שֶׁשְּׁכִינָתְךָ נוֹסַעַת עִם עַמֶּךָ.

Baruch atah, Adonai, sheSh'chinat'cha nosaat im amecha.

Praised are You, Adonai, Your Presence journeys with
Your people.

May it be Your will, Adonai our God, and God of our ancestors, that You lead us toward peace and direct our footsteps toward peace, and that You guide us toward peace and lead us to our desired destination—to life, joy, and peace.

May You send blessing on everything we do, and give us grace, favor, and mercy in Your sight and in the sight of all who behold us.

Hear our voice in prayer, for You are a God who hearkens to supplication and prayer.

בָּרוּךְ אַתָּה, יְיָ, שׁוֹמֵעַ תְּפִלָּה.

Baruch atah, Adonai, shomei-a t'filah.

Praised are You, Adonai, who hearkens to prayer.

Meditation for an Individual

God within and beyond me, Your Presence pervades the world. Wherever I go, You are near to me. "If I take up the wings of the morning, and dwell on the ocean's farthest shore, even there Your hand will lead me, Your strong hand will hold me."

(PSALM 139:9–10)

Now that I begin a new journey, I turn with confidence and trust. May I go forth in health and safely reach my destination. May this journey not be in vain; let its purpose be fulfilled; let me return in contentment to my home and my dear ones. Then will my travels be truly blessed. Amen.

Shabbat Service prior to the Trip

Adonai said to Abram, "Go forth from your native land and from your father's house to the land that I will show you. I will make of you a great nation, and I will bless you; I will make your name great, and you shall be a blessing."

(GENESIS 12:1–2)

Mi Shebeirach on Behalf of One Traveling to Israel

May the One who blessed our ancestors Abraham, Isaac, and Jacob, Sarah, Rebecca, Rachel, and Leah, bless and watch over _____, who is about to fulfill the mitzvah of visiting the Land of Israel (together with his/her family).

May you journey there safely and reach your destinations in the Land of Israel in peace. May you return safely to us. May our and God's blessings be with you as you journey through the land of our ancestors, where our brothers and sisters today strive to rebuild and revitalize the Holy Land.

May the Holy One of blessing deliver you from all trouble and distress. May you find blessing and success in all you undertake, together with all Israel, finding inspiration and renewal in our people and our Land, and let us say: Amen.

Mi Shebeirach Recited by the Traveler to Israel

May the One who blessed our ancestors Abraham, Isaac, and Jacob, Sarah, Rebecca, Rachel, and Leah, bless me (and my family) and all those with whom I am about to fulfill the mitzvah of visiting the Land of Israel.

May I [we] journey there safely and reach my [our] destinations in the Land of Israel in peace. May I [we] return safely.

May God's blessings be with me [us] as I [we] journey through the land of my [our] ancestors, where our brothers and sisters today strive to rebuild and revitalize the Holy Land.

May the Holy One of blessing deliver me [us] from all trouble and distress. May I [we] find blessing and success in all I [we] undertake, together with all Israel, finding inspiration and renewal in my [our] people and our Land, and let us say: Amen.

T'filat HaDerech – The Traveler's Prayer

תְּפִלַּת הַדֶּרֶךְ

Y'hi ratzon milfanecha	יְהִי רָצוֹן מִלְּפָנֶיךָ
Adonai Eloheinu v'Elohei	יְיָ אֱלֹהֵינוּ וֵאלֹהֵי
avoteinu v'imoteinu,	אֲבוֹתֵינוּ וְאִמּוֹתֵינוּ,
shetolicheinu	שֶׁתּוֹלִיכֵנוּ
l'shalom v'taazreinu	לְשָׁלוֹם וְתַעַזְרֵנוּ
l'hagia limchoz cheftzeinu	לְהַגִּיעַ לִמְחוֹז חֶפְצֵנוּ
l'chayim ul'simchah	לְחַיִּים וּלְשִׂמְחָה
ul'shalom.	וּלְשָׁלוֹם,
Ush'mor tzeiteinu uvo-einu	וּשְׁמֹר צֵאתֵנוּ וּבוֹאֵנוּ
v'tatzileinu mikol tzarah	וְתַצִּילֵנוּ מִכָּל צָרָה
v'tishlach b'rachah	וְתִשְׁלַח בְּרָכָה
b'chol maasei yadeinu,	בְּכָל מַעֲשֵׂי יָדֵינוּ,
umaaseinu y'chab'du	וּמַעֲשֵׂינוּ יְכַבְּדוּ

et sh'mecha. אֶת שְׁמֶךָ.

Baruch atah, Adonai, בָּרוּךְ אַתָּה, יְיָ,

shomeir Yisrael laad. שׁוֹמֵר יִשְׂרָאֵל לָעַד.

May it be Your will, our God and God of our ancestors,
that You lead us in peace
and help us reach our destination
safely, joyfully, and peacefully.
May You protect us on our leaving and on our return,
and rescue us from any harm,
and may You bless the work of our hands,
and may our deeds merit honor for You.
Praise are You, Adonai, Protector of Israel.

———————————●———————————

T'filat HaDerech

May we be blessed as we go on our way.
May we be guided in peace.
May we be blessed with health and joy.
May this be our blessing, Amen.
May we be sheltered by the wings of peace.
May we be kept in safety and in love.
May grace and compassion find their way to every soul.
May this be our blessing. Amen.

(DEBBIE FRIEDMAN)

At the Time of Departure

For a Trip to Israel

I rejoiced when they said to me, "Let us go the House of Adonai." Soon our feet shall stand within your gates, O Jerusalem. Jerusalem, a city that is bound up within itself. There the tribes of Israel would make pilgrimage, as was enjoined upon us, as the place to offer our thanks to God. In Jerusalem were set thrones of judgment, the thrones of the House of David.

> We pray for the peace of Jerusalem:
> May those that love her prosper.
> Let peace be within her ramparts,
> prosperity within her citadels.
> For the sake of my kin and companions,
> I say, "Let there be peace within her!"
> For the sake of all God's children,
> I will seek Jerusalem's well-being.

(BASED ON PSALM 122)

For Individuals, Families, and Congregations Traveling to Israel for the First Time

Behold I am about to fulfill the mitzvah of traveling to the Land of Israel, birthplace of my people and my faith.

God and God of my/our ancestors, I am returning to the birthplace of my people, the homeland of my faith, a land that is mine, yet which I have never before visited. May my journey to the Land of Israel inspire me with passion for my faith and my people. Let my travels in the Holy Land establish for me new bonds of hope and friendship.

May this journey be one not merely of the body but especially of the spirit. And may the half-remembered places, people, and events of the Land of Israel come alive before me, and may these reinvigorated memories remain strong and inspire my further learning and participation in the life of my people Israel. May this be but a first sojourn through the land of my most ancient ancestors, and may it inspire me to return yet again. Amen.

———————————•———————————

L'chi Lach

L'chi lach to a land that I will show you,
Lech l'cha to a place you do not know,
Lech l'cha, on your journey I will bless you,
And you shall be a blessing, you shall be a blessing,
You shall be a blessing, l'chi lach.
Lech l'cha, and I shall make your name great,
Lech l'cha, and all shall praise your name,
Lech l'cha, to the place that I will show you,
L'simchat chayim (3x), l'chi lach.

(DEBBIE FRIEDMAN)

For Annual or Frequent Travelers to Israel

God and God of my/our ancestors, I am returning once again to the birthplace of my people, the homeland of my faith. May I renew the bonds of common endeavor and friendship that I have fashioned there before.

May my efforts and endeavors be successful and bring me [and mine]

For a business trip:	prosperity and well-being.
For a pilgrimage:	spiritual enlightenment and well-being.
For vacation:	renewal and well-being.

And let this journey bring me new experiences and encounters, new bonds of hope and connection with the Land of Israel and its peoples.

May my journey to the Land of Israel inspire me with passion for my people, its land, and our faith.

May this journey be one not merely of the body but especially of the spirit.

And may the places, people, and events of the Land of Israel come alive before me once again, reinvigorating memories and inspiring my further learning and participation in the life of my people Israel.

And may I merit to return yet again in health and well-being. Amen.

See also *T'filat HaDerech* on pages 8–9.

2 PRAYERS UPON ARRIVING IN ISRAEL

Upon First Setting Foot in Israel

Baruch atah, Adonai
Eloheinu, Melech haolam,
hameichin mitzadei gaver.

בָּרוּךְ אַתָּה, יְיָ
אֱלֹהֵינוּ, מֶלֶךְ הָעוֹלָם,
הַמֵּכִין מִצְעֲדֵי גָבֶר.

Praised are You, Adonai our God, Sovereign of the universe, who makes firm our steps.

בָּרוּךְ אַתָּה, יְיָ אֱלֹהֵינוּ, מֶלֶךְ הָעוֹלָם, הַגּוֹמֵל
לְחַיָּבִים טוֹבוֹת, שֶׁגְּמָלַנִי כָּל טוֹב.

Baruch atah, Adonai Eloheinu, Melech haolam, hagomeil
l'chayavim tovot, sheg'malani kol tov.

Praised are You, Adonai our God, Sovereign of the universe, who has bestowed every goodness upon me.

Those hearing the words above respond:

אָמֵן. מִי שֶׁגְּמָלֵךְ/שֶׁגְּמָלְךָ כָּל טוֹב, הוּא יִגְמָלְךָ
כָּל טוֹב סֶלָה.

Amen. Mi sheg'maleich/sheg'mal'cha kol tov, hu yigmolcha kol
tov selah.

Amen. May the One who has bestowed goodness upon you continue to bestow every goodness upon you forever.

בָּרוּךְ אַתָּה, יְיָ אֱלֹהֵינוּ, מֶלֶךְ הָעוֹלָם,
שֶׁהֶחֱיָנוּ וְקִיְּמָנוּ וְהִגִּיעָנוּ לַזְּמַן הַזֶּה.

Baruch atah, Adonai Eloheinu, Melech haolam,
shehecheyanu v'kiy'manu v'higianu laz'man hazeh.

Praised are You, Adonai our God, Sovereign of the universe, for granting us life, for sustaining us, and for helping us to reach this day.

Meditation for a Group

On this soil sacred to memory, in the millennial home of our people, we offer grateful thanks for our safe arrival and pray for the welfare of this land:

Eternal God, our Rock and Redeemer, You have brought us here in peace. Now we pray, grant peace and blessing to the State of Israel, created as a haven for the oppressed and as the fulfillment of a dream. Inspire its leaders and citizens with faithfulness to the aims of its founders: to develop the land for the benefit of all its inhabitants and to implement the prophetic ideals of liberty and justice. May they live in harmony with one another and in peace with their neighbors. Help our people to realize the ancient vision that "out of Zion shall go forth Torah and the word of God from Jerusalem." (ISAIAH 2:3)

Before Retiring on a First Night in Israel

בָּרוּךְ אַתָּה, יְיָ, הַמְחַדֵּשׁ יָמֵינוּ כְּקֶדֶם.

Baruch atah, Adonai, ham'chadeish yameinu k'kedem.

Praised are You, Adonai, who renews our days as of old.

This whole land belongs to me sleeping and awake I see
one long electric flash of a dream making
flocks of swallows flutter on the tree boughs
weaving the window and my flesh and bones onto
a dizzy wind over an immense land
which all belongs to me.

(AMIR GILBOA)

My heart, homeland, is with your dews,
at night on fields of bramble,
and to the cypress's scent, and moist thistle,
I will extend a hidden wing.
Your paths are soft cradles of sand
stretching between acacia hedges,
as though on a surface of pure silk
I'll move forever upon them
held by some unfathomable charm,
and transparent skies whisper over
the dark   a frozen sea of trees.

(ESTHER RAAB)

PRAYERS AND READINGS FOR VISITING SPECIAL SITES

Jerusalem

Upon Seeing Jerusalem for the First Time

Let your presence be manifest in Jerusalem, Your city. Establish peace in her gates and quietness in the hearts of all who dwell there. Let Your Torah go forth from Zion, Your word from Jerusalem.

Baruch atah, Adonai,

בָּרוּךְ אַתָּה, יְיָ,

boneh Y'rushalayim.

בּוֹנֵה יְרוּשָׁלָיִם.

Praised are You, Adonai, Builder of Jerusalem.

From Atop Mount Scopus

From the peak of Mount Scopus,
"Shalom," Jerusalem!
From the peak of Mount Scopus,
I bow down low before you.
A hundred generations I have dreamed of you,
Dreamed of the privilege to bask in your light.
Jerusalem, Jerusalem! Smile on your children.
Jerusalem, Jerusalem! Out of your ruins will I rebuild you!

(AVIGDOR HAMEIRI)

(See full text and Hebrew on pages 84–85)

From *Y'rushalayim Shel Zahav* (Jerusalem of Gold)

The mountain air is clear as wine
and the fragrance of pine
is carried in the evening breeze
with the sound of bells.
In the slumber of tree and stone,
Captive within her dream,
is the city which sits deserted
and the wall at its heart.
Jerusalem of gold, of bronze, and of light
Am I not a harp for all your songs?

(NAOMI SHEMER)

(See full text and Hebrew on pages 85–88)

A Kavanah for Personal Renewal upon Seeing Jerusalem

We pray to stand upright, we fallen;
to be healed, we sufferers;
we pray to break the bonds
that keep us from the world of beauty;
we pray for opened eyes,
with which to see our own authentic selves.

Baruch atah, Adonai בָּרוּךְ אַתָּה, יְיָ

Eloheinu, Melech haolam, אֱלֹהֵינוּ, מֶלֶךְ הָעוֹלָם,

pokei-ach ivrim.   פּוֹקֵחַ עִוְרִים.

Praised are You, Adonai our God, Sovereign of the universe, who opens unseeing eyes.

To Jerusalem

One does not travel to Jerusalem
One returns
One ascends
the road taken by generations,
the path of longing
on the way to redemption.
One brings rucksacks
stuffed with memories
to each mountain
and each hill.
In the cobbled white alleyways
one offers a blessing
for memories of the past
which have been renewed.
One does not travel to Jerusalem.
One returns.

(YITZHAK YASINOWITZ)

———————●———————

THE LAND OF ISRAEL BY FOOT

I am the kind of person who receives feeling through their feet,
not through words or slogans; not through tradition and not
through history—only by foot. You need to walk to breathe in
the scents, absorb the colors—this is how meaning is created.
Perhaps this is the reason why I didn't want to go down to the
desert. I know my legs, I know what they can do; maybe they
don't walk as fast or as far as they used to, but they still sense,
and transfer feelings. I knew that if I walk the desert trails, that
it will come to me. Something, in fact, came to me—straight to

my mind from my feet. I've been inflicted with the plague of the nomad—and now, I am here.

(AMOS KEINAN)

Upon Entering the Old City

A Song of Ascents.
When Adonai restores the fortunes of Zion, we see it as
in a dream,
our mouths shall be filled with laughter,
our tongues, with songs of joy.
Then shall they say among the nations, "Adonai has done
great things for them!" Adonai will do great things for us
and we shall rejoice.
Restore our fortunes, Adonai, like watercourses in the
Negev.
They who sow in tears shall reap with songs of joy.
Those who go forth weeping, carrying the seed-bag,
shall come back with songs of joy, carrying their sheaves.

(PSALM 126)

The Kotel and Robinson's Arch

Eternal God, Source of our being, show compassion for Israel Your people, Jerusalem Your city, and Zion, the ancient dwelling place of Your Presence and the Mount where the Temple that bore Your name once stood….

Cause us to see the consolation of Zion, Your city, and the completion of the rebuilding of Jerusalem, Your holy city, for You are the Author of deliverance and consolation….

Let the rebuilding of Jerusalem the holy city be completed in our time.

בָּרוּךְ אַתָּה, יְיָ, בּוֹנֵה בְרַחֲמָיו יְרוּשָׁלָיִם. אָמֵן.

Baruch atah, Adonai, boneh v'rachamav Y'rushalayim. Amen.

Praised are You, Adonai, in compassion You are rebuilding Jerusalem. Amen.

Jerusalem, June 1967

Who'd have dared shaped the thought?
That we would come again to this antique rubble,
And that some definition of ourselves would grope its way forth
From these stones?
That there was a backbone to the body of our memories,
And that we could trace that backbone here,
In this eroded rock?
That millennia would not rob us of the longing to stand here,
Precisely here,
And that sophistications would not free us of the need to exult here,
Just here,
By this bone of Jerusalem,
With the gasp of a great horn filling our ears?

(STANLEY F. CHYET)

There are hearts and there are hearts. There are stones and there are stones. There are hearts of stone, and there are stones with hearts.

(RAV KOOK, AS ADAPTED BY JULIE SILVER)

The Paratroopers' Cry

This Wall has heard many prayers
This Wall has seen the fall of many other Walls.
This Wall has felt the Touch of mourning women
This Wall has felt the petitions lodged between its stones.
This Wall saw Rabbi Yehuda Halevi trampled before it
This Wall has seen Caesars rise and fall
But this wall has never seen paratroopers cry.

This Wall saw them tired and wrung out
This Wall saw them wounded and mutilated
Running to it with excitement, cries, and silence
And creeping as torn creatures in the alleys of the Old City
As they are covered with dust and with parched lips
They whisper, "If I forget thee, if I forget thee, Jerusalem."

How does it happen that paratroopers cry?
How does it happen that they touch the wall with great
    emotions?
How does it happen that their weeping changes to song?
Perhaps because these boys of nineteen, born at the same
    time as the state,
Perhaps because these boys of nineteen carry on their
    shoulders—two thousand years.

(CHAIM HEFER)

THE WALL

The wall...At first I am stunned. Then I see: a Wall of frozen tears, a cloud of sighs.

Palimpsests, hiding books, secret names. The stones are seals.

The Wall...The old mother crying for all of us. Stubborn, loving, waiting for redemption. The ground on which I stand is Amen. My words become echoes. All of our history is waiting here....

Suddenly ancient anticipations are resurrected in me. Centuries went and came. Then a moment arrived and stood still, facing me.

Once you have lived a moment at the Wall, you never go away.

(ABRAHAM JOSHUA HESCHEL)

Tzelofhad's Daughters

The five daughters of Tzelofhad,
Mahlah, Noah, Hoglah, Milcah, Tirtzah
Strong Bible women, sisters,
Stood together, sand between toes,
Toe to toe with their male elders,
Just in sight of the Promised Land.

Our father died and left no sons.
Give us our inheritance! They insisted.
Moses, confused, did not know what to do,
Except to simply ask
God, who said,
The plea is just!

Give them their share.
And it was made so.
In the Torah, it is written.

Now the great great-granddaughters of centuries of
Daughters of Tzelofhad, grown women with daughters,
And granddaughters of their own
Stand before the stones of
The Western Wall, what remains of the great Temple.
These are Women of the Wall.
They tender prayers to God
And plead their case.
Give us our share, our place before the Wall,
To pray freely, as full Jews,
This is our inheritance!

But those who rule do not ask God what is just,
Will not think to listen for
God's answer, instead
Allow the pitch of chairs,
Prayer books ripped from mothers' hands,
Allow the din of curses raining down
Upon the daughters of the hot desert sands.

(ABBY CAPLIN)

Silent sit on the ground
The elders of Fair Zion;
They have strewn dust on their heads
And girded themselves with sackcloth;
The maidens of Jerusalem have bowed
Their heads to the ground.
My eyes are spent with tears,

My heart is in tumult,
My being melts away
Over the ruin of my poor people,
As babes and sucklings languish
In the squares of the city.
They keep asking their mothers,
"Where is bread and wine?"
As they languish like battle-wounded
In the squares of the town,
As their life runs out
In their mothers' bosoms.
What can I take as witness or liken
To you, O Fair Jerusalem?
What can I match with you to console you,
O Fair Maiden Zion?
For your ruin is vast as the sea:
Who can heal you?

(LAMENTATIONS 2:10–13)

Har Herzl

יִזְכּוֹר Yizkor… we remember.

Remember our people who could not escape past
tyranny and hate;
may their memory be more than a distant shadow.
   For their dreams left unfulfilled and lives taken too
   soon: we remember.

Remember our brothers and sisters whose sacrifice gave
birth to the State of Israel;
may their courage be our inspiration and our strength.
   For life cut short and vision unrealized: we remember.

Remember the fallen of the Israel Defense Forces, the
victims of terror and tragedy;
may the darkness of their loss not obscure the light of
peace.

They were in love with the Land and in love with Life.

For the agony, the tears, the mothers and the fathers,
for the children who were and for the children yet to be:
we remember.

El Malei for Fallen IDF Soldiers

El malei rachamim,	אֵל מָלֵא רַחֲמִים,
shochein ba'mromim.	שׁוֹכֵן בַּמְּרוֹמִים.
Ham'tzei m'nuchah n'chonah	הַמְצֵא מְנוּחָה נְכוֹנָה
tachat kanfei haShechinah,	תַּחַת כַּנְפֵי הַשְּׁכִינָה,
b'maalot k'doshim	בְּמַעֲלוֹת קְדוֹשִׁים
ut'horim,	וּטְהוֹרִים,
k'zohar harakia mazhirim,	כְּזֹהַר הָרָקִיעַ מַזְהִירִים,
l'nishmot kol giborei ameinu,	לְנִשְׁמוֹת כָּל גִּבּוֹרֵי עַמֵּנוּ,
shemasru nafsham al	שֶׁמָּסְרוּ נַפְשָׁם עַל
g'ulat artzeinu.	גְּאֻלַּת אַרְצֵנוּ.
Ana, Baal harachamim,	אָנָּא, בַּעַל הָרַחֲמִים,
hastireim b'tzeil	הַסְתִּירֵם בְּצֵל
k'nafecha l'olamim,	כְּנָפֶיךָ לְעוֹלָמִים,

v'yitzror bitzror hachayim	וְיִצְרֹר בִּצְרוֹר־הַחַיִּים
et nishmatam.	אֶת נִשְׁמָתָם.
Adonai hu nachalatam,	יְיָ הוּא נַחֲלָתָם,
v'yanuchu b'shalom	וְיָנוּחוּ בְּשָׁלוֹם
al mishkavam.	עַל מִשְׁכָּבָם.
V'nomar, amen.	וְנֹאמַר, אָמֵן.

Fully compassionate God on high:

To the souls of those among our people
who bravely gave their lives for the redemption of our Land,
grant clear and certain rest with You
in the lofty heights of the sacred and pure
whose brightness shines like the very glow of heaven.

Source of mercy:
Forever enfold them in the embrace of Your wings;
secure their souls in eternity.

Adonai: they are Yours.
They will rest in peace.
Amen.

———————————●———————————

Standing here at the graves
of the visionaries, founders, leaders,
and the fallen defenders of the Jewish Homeland,
I pray that their example will inspire me
in both my learning and my deeds.
Let me not be indifferent or ignorant
of my people's history,
nor of the many individuals

who have struggled, persevered, and sacrificed
so that the State of Israel might be born anew
and fulfill the vision of our prophets
to become a light unto the nations.
For their efforts were not only on behalf
of the State of Israel,
but also for me and the entire House of Israel
throughout the world.

At the Grave of Hannah Senesh or Others

Blessed is the match consumed in kindling flame.
Blessed is the flame that burns in the secret fastness of
 the heart.
Blessed is the heart with strength to stop its beating for
 honor's sake.
Blessed is the match consumed in kindling flame.

(HANNAH SENESH)

There are stars up above,
so far away we only see their light
long, long after the star itself is gone.
And so it is with people that we loved—
their memories keep shining ever brightly
though their time with us is done.
But the stars that light up the darkest night,
these are the lights that guide us.
As we live our days, these are the ways we remember.

(HANNAH SENESH)

Upon Exiting Yad Vashem

El Malei for for the Six Million

El malei rachamim,	אֵל מָלֵא רַחֲמִים,
shochein bamromim.	שׁוֹכֵן בַּמְּרוֹמִים.
Hamtzei m'nucha n'chona	הַמְצֵא מְנוּחָה נְכוֹנָה
tachat kanfei haShechinah,	תַּחַת כַּנְפֵי הַשְּׁכִינָה,
b'maalot k'doshim	בְּמַעֲלוֹת קְדוֹשִׁים
u't'horim,	וּטְהוֹרִים,
k'zohar harakia mazhirim,	כְּזֹהַר הָרָקִיעַ מַזְהִירִים,
et nishmot shishah milyon	אֶת נִשְׁמוֹת שִׁשָּׁה־מִלְיוֹן
acheinu v'ach'yoteinu	אַחֵינוּ וְאַחְיוֹתֵינוּ
shenehergu al	שֶׁנֶּהֶרְגוּ עַל
kiddush haShem.	קִדּוּשׁ הַשֵּׁם.
Baal harachamim yastireim	בַּעַל הָרַחֲמִים יַסְתִּירֵם
b'seter k'nafav l'olamim,	בְּסֵתֶר כְּנָפָיו לְעוֹלָמִים,
v'yitzror bitzror	וְיִצְרוֹר בִּצְרוֹר
hachayim et nishmatam.	הַחַיִּים אֶת נִשְׁמָתָם.
Adonai hu nachalatam,	יְיָ הוּא נַחֲלָתָם,
v'yanuchu b'shalom	וְיָנוּחוּ בְּשָׁלוֹם
al mishkavam.	עַל מִשְׁכָּבָם.
V'nomar, amen.	וְנֹאמַר, אָמֵן.

Fully compassionate God on high:

To our six million brothers and sisters
murdered because they were Jews,
grant clear and certain rest with You
in the lofty heights of the sacred and pure
whose brightness shines like the very glow of heaven.

Source of mercy:
Forever enfold them in the embrace of Your wings;
secure their souls in eternity.

Adonai: they are Yours.
They will rest in peace.
Amen.

Kaddish L'Yom HaShoah—Shoah *Kaddish*

Auschwitz	יִתְגַּדַּל
Lodz	וְיִתְקַדַּשׁ
Ponar	שְׁמֵהּ רַבָּא,
Babi Yar	בְּעָלְמָא דִּי בְרָא כִרְעוּתֵהּ,
Maidanek	וְיַמְלִיךְ מַלְכוּתֵהּ
Birkenau	בְּחַיֵּיכוֹן וּבְיוֹמֵיכוֹן
Kovno	וּבְחַיֵּי דְכָל בֵּית יִשְׂרָאֵל,
Ianowska	בַּעֲגָלָא וּבִזְמַן קָרִיב,
	וְאִמְרוּ: אָמֵן.

יְהֵא שְׁמֵהּ רַבָּא מְבָרַךְ לְעָלַם וּלְעָלְמֵי עָלְמַיָּא.

Theresienstadt   יִתְבָּרַךְ וְיִשְׁתַּבַּח

Buchenwald   וְיִתְפָּאַר וְיִתְרוֹמַם

Treblinka   וְיִתְנַשֵּׂא וְיִתְהַדָּר

Vilna   וְיִתְעַלֶּה וְיִתְהַלָּל

Bergen-Belsen   שְׁמֵהּ דְּקֻדְשָׁא, בְּרִיךְ הוּא,

Mauthausen   לְעֵלָּא

Dachau   מִן כָּל בִּרְכָתָא וְשִׁירָתָא,

Minsk   תֻּשְׁבְּחָתָא וְנֶחֱמָתָא

Warsaw   דַּאֲמִירָן בְּעָלְמָא,

וְאִמְרוּ: אָמֵן.

יְהֵא שְׁלָמָא רַבָּא מִן־שְׁמַיָּא וְחַיִּים עָלֵינוּ
וְעַל כָּל יִשְׂרָאֵל, וְאִמְרוּ: אָמֵן.
עֹשֶׂה שָׁלוֹם בִּמְרוֹמָיו, הוּא יַעֲשֶׂה שָׁלוֹם עָלֵינוּ
וְעַל כָּל יִשְׂרָאֵל, וְאִמְרוּ: אָמֵן.

Why did heavens not darken?
Why did the stars not withdraw their brightness?
Why did they not darken in their cloud cover
when one thousand one hundred holy souls were killed
and slaughtered on one day,
on the third day of Sivan, a Tuesday—
infants and sucklings who never transgressed

and never sinned,
and poor and innocent souls?
At such things will you restrain yourself, Adonai?

(ADAPTED FROM THE CRUSADE CHRONICLE OF SOLOMON BAR-SIMSON)

●

In the presence of eyes
which witnessed the slaughter,
which saw the oppression
the heart could not bear,
and as witness the heart
that once taught compassion
until the days came to pass
that crushed human feeling,
I have taken an oath: To remember it all,
to remember—not once to forget!
Forget not one thing to the last generation
when degradation shall cease,
to the last, to its ending,
when the rod of instruction
shall have come to conclusion.
An oath: Not in vain passed over the night of terror.
An oath: No morning shall see me at flesh-pots again.
An oath: Lest from this we learned nothing.

(AVRAHAM SHLONSKY)

Tel Aviv

Above a balcony
a stretch of sea smiles at me.
Each day the wind strikes
my cheeks with the puffy hands of a baby—

beside me a stretch of sea
rests like a baby's dewy, curly head of hair
and like it, strange and rising from my flesh,
the stretch of sea smiles before me.

(ESTHER RAAB)

And now Judaism finds that it can no longer tolerate the *galut*
form which it had to take on, in obedience to its will-to-live,
when it was exiled from its own country, and that if it loses
that form its life is in danger. So it seeks to return to its historic
center, in order to live there a life of natural development, to
bring its powers into play in every department of human culture, to develop and perfect those national possessions which it
has acquired up to now, and thus to contribute to the common
stock of humanity, in the future as in the past, a great national
culture, the fruit of the unhampered activity of a people living
according to its own spirit. For this purpose Judaism needs at
present but little. It needs not an independent State, but only the
creation in its native land of conditions favorable to its development: a good-sized settlement of Jews working *without hindrance*
in every branch of culture, from agriculture and handicrafts to
science and literature. This Jewish settlement, which will be a
gradual growth, will become in course of time the center of the
nation, wherein its spirit will find pure expression and develop
in all its aspects up to the highest degree of perfection of which
it is capable. Then from this center the spirit of Judaism will
go forth to the great circumference, to all the communities of
the Diaspora, and will breathe new life into them and preserve
their unity; and when our national culture in Palestine has at-
tained that level, we may be confident that it will produce men

---

in the country who will be able, on a favorable opportunity, to establish a State which will be a *Jewish* State, and not merely a State of Jews.

(AHAD HA'AM, 1887, BURIED IN TRUMPLEDOR CEMETERY IN TEL AVIV)

Rabin Square or the Rabin Museum

EXCERPT FROM LAST REMARKS BY LATE PRIME MINISTER RABIN AT TEL AVIV PEACE RALLY, NOVEMBER 4, 1995

But, more than anything, in the more than three years of this Government's existence, the Israeli people has proven that it is possible to make peace, that peace opens the door to a better economy and society; that peace is not just a prayer. Peace is first of all in our prayers, but it is also the aspiration of the Jewish people, a genuine aspiration for peace....

Without partners for peace, there can be no peace. We will demand that they do their part for peace, just as we will do our part for peace, in order to solve the most complicated, prolonged, and emotionally charged aspect of the Israeli-Arab conflict: the Palestinian-Israeli conflict.

This is a course which is fraught with difficulties and pain. For Israel, there is no path that is without pain. But the path of peace is preferable to the path of war. I say this to you as one who was a military man, someone who is today Minister of Defense and sees the pain of the families of the IDF soldiers. For them, for our children, in my case for our grandchildren, I want this Government to exhaust every opening, every possibility, to promote and achieve a comprehensive peace. Even with Syria, it will be possible to make peace.

This rally must send a message to the Israeli people, to the Jewish people around the world, to the many people in the Arab world, and indeed to the entire world, that the Israeli people want peace, support peace. For this, I thank you.

After these remarks, and right before he was shot, Rabin sang "Shir LaShalom," the words to which can be found on pages 88–90.

Independence Hall

FROM ISRAEL'S DECLARATION OF INDEPENDENCE

[The State of Israel] will foster the development of the country for the benefit of all its inhabitants; it will be based on freedom, justice, and peace as envisaged by the prophets of Israel; it will ensure complete equality of social and political rights to all its inhabitants irrespective of religion, race, or sex; it will guarantee freedom of religion, conscience, language, education, and culture; it will safeguard the Holy Places of all religions; and it will be faithful to the principles of the Charter of the United Nations.

———————●———————

Are we to ask merely for the right of asylum
in our historic home,
the right which any people may claim
in any part of the world,
though, unfortunately, such claims are
only infrequently recognized?
Is this Jewish statesmanship?
Is this Jewish vision, courage, faith?
Or are we to declare in this great assembly,
when the proper time comes, that we stand by those
who have given their tears and their blood and their sweat
to build for them and for us and the future generations,
at long last, after the weary centuries,

a home, a National Home, a Jewish Commonwealth
where the spirit of our entire people can finally be at rest
as well as the people itself?

(ABBA HILLEL SILVER)

Caesarea

Eli Eli (*Halichah L'Keisariah*)

Eli Eli, shelo yigameir l'olam:
Hachol v'hayam, rishrush shel hamayim,
B'rak hashamayim, t'filat haadam.

O God, my God, I pray that these things never end:
The sand and the sea, the rush of the waters,
The crash of the heavens, the prayer of the heart.

(HANNAH SENESH)

Tzfat

Tzfat

Now I understand why the mystics came here:
To settle questions that caused
a great trembling for their generation
(and our generation, and others to come).
It is the nights,
spread like a midnight blue comforter
throughout the Galilee,
stretched at your feet.
It is the endless display of stars,
and a mid-month moon, and orchestrated sounds,
full of mysteries.

The mountains are lush with patterns.
The sea, at a distance, near dusk,
is the color of primeval tzitzis.
Here, on the hill, the world is a veil
of lyrics stunning your senses;
upper and lower spheres merge at every glance.
Four hundred years ago
they made note of secrets in secret language,
and laws, and walked through the fields
to greet the Sabbath Bride,
so real they circled her in dance.
Now they are painters.
The touch of brushes
makes new fires to enchant us.
Here, too, are the graves
of the Ma'alot children.
Surely, when the footsteps of the Messiah
will be heard in the Land,
the resurrection of the dead
will begin here.
Strolling the summer hillsides,
I see a great rebirth is at hand.

(DANNY SIEGEL)

The Kinneret

בָּרוּךְ אַתָּה, יְיָ אֱלֹהֵינוּ, מֶלֶךְ הָעוֹלָם,
הַמּוֹצִיא מַיִם חַיִּים.

Baruch atah, Adonai Eloheinu, Melech haolam,
hamotzi mayim chayim.

Praised are You, Adonai our God, Sovereign of the
universe, who causes living waters to flow forth.

Kinneret

There, the heights of the Golan, you would caress them
by stretching out a hand,
suggest a serene and silent pause,
there, the venerable Hermon,
in its radiant solitude,
the immaculate crown
sends me its wind.
There, on the lake shore, a small palm tree
with its tousled branches
like a mischievous child
running along the lake shore to dip his feet
into the waters of Kinneret.

(RACHEL BLAUSTEIN)

Perhaps

Perhaps these things have never been at all!
Perhaps that life was not!
Perhaps I never answered morning's earliest call
To sweat in labor on my garden plot!
Perhaps I never stood upon the loaded cart
To gather up the hay,
Nor heard the wild songs bursting from my heart
the livelong harvest day!
Perhaps I never made my body whole

In the blue and quiet gleam
Of my Kineret! Oh, Kineret of my soul,
Were you once true, or have I dreamed a dream?

(RACHEL BLAUSTEIN)

The Kinneret is not simply a landscape, not just a part of nature; the fate of a people is contained in its name. Our past peeks out of it to watch us with thousands of eyes; with thousands of mouths it communicates with our hearts.

(RACHEL BLAUSTEIN)

The Dead Sea

THE PROPHECY OF EZEKIEL

"Do you see, O mortal?" he said to me; and he led me back to the bank of the stream.

As I came back, I saw trees in great profusion on both banks of the stream. "This water," he told me, "runs out to the eastern region, and flows into the Aravah; and when it comes into the sea, into the sea of foul waters [the Dead Sea], the water will become wholesome. Every living creature that swarms will be able to live wherever this stream goes.…"

(EZEKIEL 47:6–9)

Ein Gedi

בָּרוּךְ אַתָּה, יְיָ אֱלֹהֵינוּ, מֶלֶךְ הָעוֹלָם,
הַמְשַׁלֵּחַ מַעְיָנִים בַּנְּחָלִים.

Baruch atah, Adonai Eloheinu, Melech haolam,
ham'shalei-ach mayanim ban'chalim.

Praised are You, Adonai our God, Sovereign of the
universe, who makes springs gush forth in torrents.

(BASED ON PSALM 104:10)

For Other Bodies of Water

A Spring-Fed Stream

בָּרוּךְ אַתָּה, יְיָ אֱלֹהֵינוּ, מֶלֶךְ הָעוֹלָם,
יַנְחִילֵנוּ עַל מַבּוּעֵי מָיִם.

Baruch atah, Adonai Eloheinu, Melech haolam,
yanchileinu al mabu-ei mayim.

Praised are You, Adonai our God, Sovereign of the
universe, who guides us to springs of water.

(ISAIAH 49:10)

The Mediterranean Sea or the Gulf of Aqaba/Eilat

בָּרוּךְ אַתָּה, יְיָ אֱלֹהֵינוּ, מֶלֶךְ הָעוֹלָם,
שֶׁעָשָׂה אֶת הַיָּם הַגָּדוֹל.

Baruch atah, Adonai Eloheinu, Melech haolam,
she-asah et hayam hagadol.

Praised are You, Adonai our God, Sovereign of the
universe, Maker of the great seas.

For Mountains

בָּרוּךְ אַתָּה, יְיָ אֱלֹהֵינוּ, מֶלֶךְ הָעוֹלָם, יוֹצֵר הָרִים.

Baruch atah, Adonai Eloheinu, Melech haolam, yotzeir harim.

Praised are You, Adonai our God, Sovereign of the universe, who forms mountains.

(BASED ON AMOS 4:13)

———————●———————

A Song of Ascent—
I lift up my eyes to the hills.
What is the source my help?
My help comes from Adonai,
Maker of the heavens and the earth.
God will not allow you to stumble,
your Guardian will not slumber.
Indeed, the Guardian of Israel
neither slumbers nor sleeps.
Adonai is your Guardian,
your shelter at your side.
The sun will not smite you by day
nor the moon by night.
Adonai will guard you against all evil;
God will guard you, body and soul.
Adonai will guard your going out
and your coming home, now and forever.

(PSALM 121)

———————●———————

הִנֵּה מַה־טּוֹב וּמַה־נָּעִים
שֶׁבֶת אַחִים גַּם־יָחַד.
כְּטַל־חֶרְמוֹן שֶׁיֹּרֵד עַל־הַרְרֵי צִיּוֹן.

Hineih mah tov umah na-im
shevet achim gam yachad.
K'tal Chermon sheyoreid al har'rei Tziyon.

How good and pleasant it is
that siblings dwell together…
like the dew of Mount Hermon
that falls upon the mountains of Zion.

(PSALM 133:1, 3)

Masada

בָּרוּךְ אַתָּה, יְיָ אֱלֹהֵינוּ, מֶלֶךְ הָעוֹלָם,
שֶׁכָּכָה לוֹ בְּעוֹלָמוֹ.

Baruch atah, Adonai Eloheinu, Melech haolam,
shekakah lo b'olamo.

Praised are You, Adonai our God, Sovereign of the
universe, who has created such wonders in the world.

●

בָּרוּךְ אַתָּה, יְיָ אֱלֹהֵינוּ, מֶלֶךְ הָעוֹלָם, שֶׁהֶעֱלָה
אֶת אֲבוֹתֵינוּ וְאִמּוֹתֵינוּ עַל הֶהָרִים לִרְאוֹת אֶת
הָאָרֶץ.

Baruch atah, Adonai Eloheinu, Melech haolam, shehe-elah et
avoteinu v'imoteinu al heharim lirot et haaretz.

Praised are You, Adonai our God, Sovereign of the
universe, who enabled our ancestors ascend such heights
to view the land.

(Based on Deuteronomy 32:49)

Masada

Who are you that come, stepping heavy in silence?
—The remnant.
Alone I remained on the day of great slaughter.
Alone, of father and mother, sisters and brothers.
Saved in an empty cask hid in a courtyard corner.
Huddled, a child in the womb of an anxious mother.
I survived.
Days upon days in fate's embrace I cried and begged
for mercy:
Thy deed it is, O God, that I remain.
Then answer: Why?
If to bear the shame of man and the world.
To blazen it forever—
Release me! The world unshamed will flaunt this shame
As honor and spotless virtue!
And if to find atonement I survive
Then answer: Where?
So importuning a silent voice replied:
"In Masada!"
And I obeyed that voice and so I came.
Silent my steps will raise me to the wall,
Silent as all the steps filled with the dread
Of what will come.

Tall, tall is the wall of Masada.
Deep, deep is the pit at its feet.
And if the silent voice deceived me,
From the high wall to the deep pit
I will fling me.
And let there be no sign remaining,
And let no remnant survive.

(YITZCHAK LAMDAN)

"After 2,000 Years, a Seed from Ancient Judea Sprouts"

*A 2,000-year-old seed from a Judean date palm seed found at
the excavations of Herod's palace at Masada was successfully
germinated into a healthy tree in 2005.*

Not merely stubborn resistance,
but miraculous persistence.
The dangerous price of zealotry,
the barren beauty of isolation.
Unexpected, life amidst the strata of death.
Cultured resurrection. Suicide at last rejected.
Teach us, O God, that these too
can be the story of the fortress called Masada.

4 PRAYERS FOR UNIQUE MOMENTS IN ISRAEL

When Planting a Tree in Israel

Tree Planting Prayer

Avinu Shebashamayim,
Builder of Zion and Jerusalem,
Founder of Israel's realm.
"From the heavens,
From the Dwelling Place of Your Holiness,
Look upon and bless Your people Israel
and the land that You gave us,
a land flowing with milk and honey,
as You swore to our ancestors" (Deuteronomy 26:15).

Find favor with Your land, O God,
and infuse it with the benefit of Your loving-kindness.
Give dew for a blessing,
and cause desirable rains to fall in their time.
Satiate the mountains of Israel and its valleys,
and water in them every plant and tree.
"Saturating its furrows, leveling its ridges,
You soften it with showers, You bless its growth" (Psalm 65:11).

Deepen the roots of the plantings
that we have planted today.
Cause them to grow for the beauty
and adornment of the land,

along with all the other trees of Israel.
Cause us also to take root in the soil of our ancestors.
Raise us up with these trees for acceptance and blessing.
And through us may all the families of the earth be
blessed.
"May truth spring up from the land, and justice look
down from the heavens" (PSALM 85:12).

Amen.

When Visiting Kibbutzim or Other Agricultural Settlements

Working is another way of praying.
You plant in Israel the soul of a tree.
You plant in the desert the spirit of gardens.

Praying is another way of singing.
You plant in the tree the soul of lemons.
You plant in the gardens the spirit of roses.

Singing is another way of loving.
You plant in the lemons the spirit of your son.
You plant in the roses the soul of your daughter.

Loving is another way of living.
You plant in your daughter the spirit of Israel.
You plant in your son the soul of the desert.

(DANNIE ABSE)

———————————●———————————

God turns the wilderness into pools,
Parched land into springs of water.

There God settles the hungry;
They build a place to settle in.
They sow fields and plant vineyards
That yield a bountiful harvest.

(PSALM 107:35–37)

Where a Miracle Occurred

Days pass and the years vanish, and we walk sightless among miracles. God, fill our eyes with seeing and our minds with knowing. Let there be moments when your Presence, like lightning, illumines the darkness in which we walk. Help us to see, wherever we gaze, that the bush burns, unconsumed. And we, clay touched by God, will reach out for holiness and exclaim in wonder, "How filled with awe is this place, and we did not know it" (GENESIS 28:16).

בָּרוּךְ אַתָּה, יְיָ אֱלֹהֵינוּ, מֶלֶךְ הָעוֹלָם, שֶׁעָשָׂה
נִסִּים לַאֲבוֹתֵינוּ וְאִמּוֹתֵינוּ בַּמָּקוֹם הַזֶּה.

Baruch atah, Adonai Eloheinu, Melech haolam, she-asah nisim laavoteinu v'imoteinu bamakom hazeh.

Praised are You, Adonai our God, Sovereign of the universe, who made miracles for our ancestors in this place.

Where Idolatry Was Uprooted

Baruch atah, Adonai　　　　　　בָּרוּךְ אַתָּה, יְיָ

Eloheinu, Melech haolam,　　אֱלֹהֵינוּ, מֶלֶךְ הָעוֹלָם,

she-akar avodah zarah

שֶׁעָקַר עֲבוֹדָה זָרָה

mei-artzeinu.

מֵאַרְצֵנוּ.

Praised are You, Adonai our God, Sovereign of the universe, who uprooted idolatry from our land.

When Visiting a Grave

The dust returns to the earth as it was, but the spirit returns to God who gave it.

(ECCLESIASTES 12:7)

בָּרוּךְ אַתָּה, יְיָ אֱלֹהֵינוּ, מֶלֶךְ הָעוֹלָם, אֲשֶׁר בַּדִּין
וּבְרַחֲמִים יוֹצֵר אוֹתָנוּ, וְהַזָּן וּמְכַלְכֵּל אוֹתָנוּ,
וְמֵמִית אוֹתָנוּ, וְיוֹדֵעַ מִסְפָּר כֻּלָּנוּ, וְעָתִיד לְהַחֲזִיר
וּלְהַחֲיוֹת אוֹתָנוּ. בָּרוּךְ אַתָּה, יְיָ, מְחַיֶּה הַמֵּתִים.

Baruch atah, Adonai Eloheinu, Melech haolam, asher badin
uvarachamim yotzeir otanu, v'hazan v'm'chalkeil otanu,
v'meimit otanu, v'yodei-a mispar kulanu, v'atid l'hachazir
ul'hachayot otanu. Baruch atah, Adonai, m'chayeih hameitim.

Praised are You, Adonai our God, Sovereign of the universe, who in judgment and compassion creates us, maintains and sustains us, and who knows our number, who reviews our deeds, and who renews life. Praised are You, Adonai, who renews life.

Merciful One, I/we have come to pray at the Tomb of

_____.

Let his/her meritorious acts inspire me and stand in my
stead. Remember his/her merit and bring redemption to
the descendants of his/her people for Your name's sake.
[I pray on behalf of…] Answer my prayers and the
prayers of my fellow Jews. Listen to what I utter before
You, and fulfill my innermost needs.

בָּרוּךְ אַתָּה, יְיָ, שׁוֹמֵעַ תְּפִלָּה.

Baruch atah, Adonai, shomei-a t'filah.

Praised are You, Adonai, who hearkens to prayer.

At a Historic Synagogue

Vaani, b'rov chasd'cha	וַאֲנִי בְּרֹב חַסְדְּךָ
avo veitecha,	אָבוֹא בֵיתֶךָ,
eshtachaveh el heichal	אֶשְׁתַּחֲוֶה אֶל־הֵיכַל
kodsh'cha b'yiratecha.	קָדְשְׁךָ בְּיִרְאָתֶךָ.

As for me, O God abounding in grace, I enter Your house
to worship with awe in Your sacred place.

(PSALM 5:8)

The synagogue is the sanctuary of Israel. Born of our longing
for the living God, it has been to Israel, throughout our wan-
derings, a visible token of the presence of God in our people's
midst. Its beauty is the beauty of holiness; steadfast it has stood
as the champion of justice, mercy, and peace. Its truths are true
for all people. Its love is a love for all people. Its God is the God

of all people, as it has been said: "My house shall be called a house of prayer for all peoples" (Isaiah 56:7).

Let all the family of Israel, all who hunger for righteousness, all who seek the Eternal, find God here, and here find life!

בָּרוּךְ אַתָּה, יְיָ אֱלֹהֵינוּ, מֶלֶךְ הָעוֹלָם, שֶׁחָלַק מֵחָכְמָתוֹ לִירֵאָיו.

Baruch atah, Adonai Eloheinu, Melech haolam, shechalak meichochmato lirei-av.

Praised are You, Adonai our God, Sovereign of the universe, who shares wisdom with those who are reverent.

At an Archaeological Site, Museum, or Display of Antiquities

Atah chonein l'adam daat	אַתָּה חוֹנֵן לְאָדָם דַּעַת
um'lameid le-enosh binah.	וּמְלַמֵּד לֶאֱנוֹשׁ בִּינָה.
Choneinu mei-it'cha	חָנֵּנוּ מֵאִתְּךָ
chochmah, binah, vadaat.	חָכְמָה, בִּינָה וָדַעַת.
Baruch atah, Adonai,	בָּרוּךְ אַתָּה, יְיָ,
chonein hadaat.	חוֹנֵן הַדַּעַת.

You grace humans with knowledge
and teach mortals understanding.
Graciously share with us Your wisdom,
insight, and knowledge.
Praised are You, Adonai,
who graces us with knowledge.

Ancient One of old, guide me now, in this place, to see
and understand,
not just cases and displays, not mere antiquities and
reproductions,
not simply empty vessels in array, but the remnants of
generations gone by,
the handiwork of my ancestors, still vibrant and infused
with the holiness of those who made and used them.

Open my eyes and my soul. Let me be touched by the resonance
of those who fashioned them, infuse me with the reality and
vitality of their efforts.

Renew our days as of old.

At an Archaeological Site

At an archaeological site
I saw fragments of precious vessels, well cleaned
and groomed and oiled and spoiled.
And beside it I saw a heap of discarded dust
which wasn't even good for thorns and thistles to grow on.
I asked: What is the gray dust which
has been pushed around and sifted
and tortured and then thrown away?

I answered in my heart: This dust
is people like us, who during their
lifetime lived separated from
copper and gold and marble stones
and all other precious things—

---

and they remained so in death.
We are this heap of dust, our
bodies, our souls, all the words
in our mouths, all hopes.

(YEHUDA AMICHAI)

When Standing at or Crossing the Borders of the State of Israel

בָּרוּךְ אַתָּה בְּבֹאֶךָ וּבָרוּךְ אַתָּה בְּצֵאתֶךָ.

Baruch atah b'vo-echa u'varuch atah b'tzeitecha.

Blessed shall you be in your comings and blessed shall
you be in your goings.

(DEUTERONOMY 28:6)

●

Behold, I am sending an angel before you to guard you on the
way and to bring you to the place that I have made ready.

(EXODUS 23:20)

●

May the Eternal bless you and protect you!
May the Eternal deal kindly and graciously with you!
May the Eternal bestow divine favor upon you and grant
you peace!

(NUMBERS 6:24–26)

●

We began to plant orchards and vineyards, to keep chickens
and turkeys, to plant and water vegetables. The place began to

hum. Hands and heads were busy all day long; the work took everything, body and mind.

Then came the years of growth. The children grew; the numbers of the cattle grew; the coops became more crowded, the summits of the fruit trees reached higher, the stocks in the vineyards spread out their nets.

(DVORAH DAYAN, ON THE EARLY DAYS OF NAHALAL)

For Participating in Acts of Social Justice

בָּרוּךְ אַתָּה, יְיָ אֱלֹהֵינוּ, מֶלֶךְ הָעוֹלָם,
שֶׁנָּתַן לָנוּ הִזְדַּמְּנוּת לְתַקֵּן אֶת הָעוֹלָם.

Baruch atah, Adonai Eloheinu, Melech haolam,
shenatan lanu hizdamnut l'takein et haolam.

Praised are You, Adonai our God, Sovereign of the universe, who has given us the opportunity to repair the world.

Don't merely expect to find or to believe that life is
worthwhile; make it worthwhile.
Don't merely see life whole; make it whole.
Not knowing which should come first,
to improve one's self or to improve the world,
we end up doing neither.
Actually, the only way to improve the world is by
improving one's self,
and the only way to improve one's self
is by improving the world.

(SOURCE UNKNOWN)

Prayers for the State of Israel and the Israel Defense Forces

For the State of Israel

Avinu Shebashamayim,	אָבִינוּ שֶׁבַּשָּׁמַיִם,
tzur Yisrael v'go-alo,	צוּר יִשְׂרָאֵל וְגוֹאֲלוֹ,
bareich et m'dinat Yisrael,	בָּרֵךְ אֶת מְדִינַת יִשְׂרָאֵל,
reishit tz'michat g'ulateinu.	רֵאשִׁית צְמִיחַת גְּאֻלָּתֵנוּ.
Hagein aleha	הָגֵן עָלֶיהָ
b'evrat chasdecha,	בְּאֶבְרַת חַסְדֶּךָ,
ufros aleha	וּפְרוֹס עָלֶיהָ
sukat sh'lomecha.	סֻכַּת שְׁלוֹמֶךָ.
Ush'lach orcha vaamit'cha	וּשְׁלַח אוֹרְךָ וַאֲמִתְּךָ
l'rasheha, sareha v'yo-atzeha,	לְרָאשֶׁיהָ, שָׂרֶיהָ וְיוֹעֲצֶיהָ,
v'takneim b'eitzah	וְתַקְּנֵם בְּעֵצָה
tovah milfanecha.	טוֹבָה מִלְּפָנֶיךָ.
Chazeik y'dei m'ginei	חַזֵּק יְדֵי מְגִנֵּי
eretz kodsheinu,	אֶרֶץ קָדְשֵׁנוּ,
v'hanchileim y'shuah v'chayim.	וְהַנְחִילֵם יְשׁוּעָה וְחַיִּים.
V'natata shalom baaretz,	וְנָתַתָּ שָׁלוֹם בָּאָרֶץ,
v'simchat olam l'yoshveha.	וְשִׂמְחַת עוֹלָם לְיוֹשְׁבֶיהָ.
Amen.	אָמֵן.

O Heavenly One, Protector and Redeemer of Israel, bless the State of Israel which marks the dawning of hope for all who seek peace. Shield it beneath the wings of Your love; spread over it the canopy of Your peace; send Your light and truth to all who lead and advise, guiding them with Your good counsel. Strengthen the hands of those who defend our holy land, grant them deliverance, and adorn them in a mantle of victory. Establish peace in the land and fullness of joy for all who dwell there. Amen.

Pray for the peace of Jerusalem; may those who love you prosper! Let there be peace in your homes, safety within your borders. For the sake of my people, my friends, I pray you find peace. For the sake of the house of the Eternal our God, I will seek your good.

(PSALM 122:6–9)

For the Israel Defense Forces

מִי שֶׁבֵּרַךְ אֲבוֹתֵינוּ, אַבְרָהָם יִצְחָק וְיַעֲקֹב,
וְאִמּוֹתֵינוּ, שָׂרָה רִבְקָה רָחֵל וְלֵאָה, הוּא יְבָרֵךְ
אֶת חַיָּלֵי צְבָא הַהֲגַנָּה לְיִשְׂרָאֵל וּשְׁאָר מָגִנֵּי
עַמֵּנוּ, הָעוֹמְדִים עַל מִשְׁמַרְתָּם. יִשְׁמְרֵם הַקָּדוֹשׁ
בָּרוּךְ הוּא וְיַצִּילֵם מִכָּל צָרָה וְצוּקָה וּמִכָּל נֶגַע
וּמַחֲלָה, וְיִשְׁלַח בְּרָכָה בְּכָל מַעֲשֵׂה יְדֵיהֶם. וִיקַיֵּם
בָּהֶם הַכָּתוּב: "וְכִתְּתוּ חַרְבוֹתֵיהֶם לְאִתִּים,
וַחֲנִיתוֹתֵיהֶם לְמַזְמֵרוֹת; לֹא יִשְׂאוּ גוֹי אֶל־גּוֹי

חֶרֶב, וְלֹא יִלְמְדוּן עוֹד מִלְחָמָה: וְיָשְׁבוּ אִישׁ
תַּחַת גַּפְנוֹ וְתַחַת תְּאֵנָתוֹ וְאֵין מַחֲרִיד"
(מיכה ד:ג): וְנֹאמַר: אָמֵן.

Mi shebeirach avoteinu Avraham, Yitzchak, v'Yaakov,
v'imoteinu, Sarah, Rivkah, Rachel, v'Leah, hu y'vareich et
chayalei tz'va hahaganah l'Yisrael ush'ar m'ginei ameinu,
haom'dim al mishmartam. Yishm'reim hakadosh baruch hu
v'yatzileim mikol tzarah v'tzukah u'mikol nega umachalah
v'yishlach b'rachah b'chol maaseih y'deihem. Vikuyam bahem
hakatuv: "V'chit'tu charvoteihem l'itim, vachanitoteihem
l'mazmeirot; lo yis'u goy el goy cherev, v'lo yil'm'dun od
milchamah: V'yash'vu ish tachat gafno v'tachat t'einato v'ein
macharid": V'nomar: Amen.

May the One who blessed our ancestors Abraham, Isaac,
and Jacob, Sarah, Rebecca, Rachel, and Leah, bless the soldiers
of Israel's Defense Forces, and all who stand guard in order to
protect our people. May the Holy One, blessed be God, protect them and save them from all troubles and afflictions, from
all sickness and injury, and send blessing to all their endeavors. May the words of the prophet come to fruition through
them: "And they shall beat their swords into ploughshares and
their spears into pruning hooks; nation shall not lift up sword
against nation, neither shall they learn war any more. And each
one shall sit under the vine and under the fig tree and none
shall be afraid (MICHA 4:3)," and let us say, Amen.

For Israeli Soldiers or Civilians Being Held Captive

Our God, the One who raised Joseph up from the pit, be "a refuge for the oppressed, a refuge in times of trouble" (PSALM 9:10).

Send complete rescue and full redemption to those held captive by the enemy: [insert names].

Strengthen their spirit and bring them our prayers that they be protected from all harm.

Implant understanding in the heart of the enemy that they may return the captives in wholeness of body and spirit.

Grant wisdom to the Israel Defense Forces that they may secure freedom for the captives without loss of life.

Grant strength of spirit and courage of heart to all the sons and daughters of Abraham, Sarah, and Hagar to release bonds of captivity and allow us all to live in freedom.

"They shall call upon Me, and I will answer them; I will be with them in distress; I will rescue them, and honor them" (ADAPTED FROM PSALM 91:15).

5 PRAYERS FOR SPECIFIC OCCASIONS

For *B'nei Mitzvah* Ceremonies in Israel

Recited by Parents Celebrating a Child's Becoming Bar/Bat Mitzvah in Israel

Into our hands, O God, You have placed Your Torah, to be held high by parents and children, and taught by one generation to the next. Whatever has befallen us, our people have remained steadfast in loyalty to the Torah. It was carried into exile in the arms of parents, that their children might not be deprived of their birthright.

Now we have journeyed to the birthplace of our people, the Land of Israel, that you might celebrate the occasion of becoming Bar/Bat Mitzvah. May our presence in the Holy Land inspire you, linking you across time and space with our ancestors and our people, their ancient words and modern yearnings. May you forever carry the memory of this day and place in your heart.

And now we pray that you, _____, may always be worthy of this inheritance. Take its teaching into your heart, and in turn pass it on to your children and those who come after you. May you be a faithful Jew, searching for wisdom and truth, working for justice and peace.

May the God of our people, the God of all humankind, bless and keep you. May the One who has always been our guide inspire you to bring honor to our family and to the House of Israel.

בָּרוּךְ אַתָּה, יְיָ אֱלֹהֵינוּ, מֶלֶךְ הָעוֹלָם, שֶׁנָּתַן לִי
אֶת הַזְּכוּת וְאֶת הַכָּבוֹד לִמְסוֹר לְךָ/לָךְ תּוֹרָה.

*Baruch atah, Adonai Eloheinu, Melech haolam, shenatan li et
haz'chut v'et hakavod limsor l'cha/lach Torah.*

Praised are You, Adonai our God, Sovereign of the
universe, who has granted me the merit and honor of
transmitting Torah to you.

Mi Shebeirach for a Bar/Bat Mitzvah in Israel

May the One who blessed our ancestors… bless _____,
daughter/son of _____, who has journeyed here today to enter into her/his own responsibility for the command-
ments of the Torah in the sight of this congregation in the Land
of Israel.

May God grant her/his parents blessing: As they merited to
raise her/him up in performing mitzvot, so too may they merit
guiding her/him to Torah, to the chuppah, and to the perfor-
mance of deeds of loving-kindness.

O Divine Parent, may it be pleasing to You, that she/he merit
to pursue Torah in health of body and wholeness of spirit, that
she/he may find favor and esteem in the sight of God and all
humanity. May her/his parents see and rejoice, her/his loved
ones exult, and all the House of Israel celebrate in jubilation.

Recited by a Bar/Bat Mitzvah in Israel

God of Israel, like Jews of generations past, I take my place today as a Bar/Bat Mitzvah.

I have journeyed with my family to the birthplace of our
people and heritage. Let me be inspired by the people, places,

and history of this Holy Land. May the memory of this day and place live on within me every day, wherever I live and wherever I journey.

Grant that I may understand my responsibility as a Jew, to show love to my family and friends, to learn more and more about the traditions of my people and my heritage, and to act with respect and compassion toward all God's children.

O God, make me grateful for all that I have, and ready always to share with those who are in need. Then I will be able to say:

I am a Jew because a hundred generations before me were steadfast in their faith. I am a Jew because the faith of Israel teaches love and kindness. I am a Jew because the faith of Israel teaches justice, compassion, and truth.

בָּרוּךְ אַתָּה, יְיָ אֱלֹהֵינוּ, מֶלֶךְ הָעוֹלָם,
שֶׁהֶחֱיָנוּ וְקִיְּמָנוּ וְהִגִּיעָנוּ לַזְּמַן הַזֶּה.

Baruch atah, Adonai Eloheinu, Melech haolam, shehecheyanu v'kiy'manu v'higianu laz'man hazeh.

Praised are You, Adonai our God, Sovereign of the universe, for giving us life, for sustaining us, and for enabling us to reach this season.

Recited by a Bar/Bat Mitzvah at a Synagogue in Israel

My God and God of my ancestors:
In the presence of this sacred congregation in the Land of Israel, I choose to be counted in the Congregation of Israel—inheriting its legacy, partner to its destiny, and obliged by the mitzvot.

Give me strength to follow Your ways and to be a source of pride to my family, to my community, and to my people Israel.

How greatly we are blessed, how good is our portion, how pleasant our lot, how beautiful our heritage.

How blessed are we that we unify Your Name and say:

שְׁמַע יִשְׂרָאֵל יְהוָה אֱלֹהֵינוּ יְהוָה אֶחָד!

Sh'ma Yisrael, Adonai Eloheinu, Adonai Echad!

Hear, O Israel, Adonai is our God, Adonai is One!

For Dedicating Resources in Israel

May the One who blessed our ancestors in every generation, bless _____ together with all who support and contribute to the well-being and prosperity of the State of Israel and its institutions: bless them, their children, their families, and all that is theirs, along with all those who devotedly involve themselves with the needs of this institution [synagogue, hospital, museum, JNF, etc.] and the State of Israel.

May the Holy One, praised be God, reward them; may God banish sickness from them, heal them, and forgive their faults. May God bless them with kindness and compassion, long life, ample sustenance, health of body, and enlightenment of the spirit. May God bless them by prospering all their worthy efforts and endeavors, as well as those of the entire people Israel. And let us say: Amen.

For Attending a Convention in Israel

Blessed is the One who discerns secrets, for the mind of each is different from the other, as is the face of each different from the other.

(BABYLONIAN TALMUD, B'RACHOT 58A)

May Your Presence dwell among us, drawing us to serve
You and Your children with love and compassion.
May we listen to each other with respect,
and treat each other with honor and generosity.
May the words we speak be for the sake of heaven.
May our eyes be open to Your Presence
in the smallest things we do.

May the favor of Adonai our God be upon us;
And let our efforts prosper.
O prosper our efforts!

(PSALM 90:17)

May it be Your will Adonai, to fill our lives with purpose and intention, love and companionship, peace and friendship. Make our habitations rich in disciples, and enrich us with hope of the future. Grant us a share in the uplifting of Your world, and sustain us in life with good companions and a worthy impulse, that we may arise and find our hearts open to Your awe-inspiring Presence. And may the longings of our souls be pleasing to You.

(ADAPTED FROM BABYLONIAN TALMUD, B'RACHOT 16B)

O God, the assembled hosts of Your people, the House of Israel, in every generation glorify Your name in song.

In joy and celebration we have traveled here to the Land of Israel fulfilling the commandment:

Assemble the people—men, women, children, and those who sojourn in your communities—that they may hear and so learn to revere Adonai your God and to observe faithfully every word of this Teaching. (DEUTERONOMY 31:12)

Bless our gathering; grant us insight and a spirit of cooperation. May our assembly here in M'dinat Yisrael—the State of Israel—inspire us with the memory and example of our ancestors and their deeds. Matriarchs and patriarchs, prophets and priests, judges and kings, heroes and heroines, sages and scholars, visionaries and founders, soldiers and politicians: may their spirit imbue us with zeal for the well-being of our spiritual homeland and all its peoples. May we return from our gathering having taken to heart the words of the prophet: "For Torah shall go forth from Zion, and the word of Adonai from Jerusalem" (ISAIAH 2:3).

Readings for Peace and Fellowship

A Prayer—
What shall I ask You for, God?
I have everything.
There's nothing I lack.
I ask only for one thing
And not for myself alone;
It's for many mothers, and children, and fathers

Not just in this land, but in many lands hostile to
  each other.
I'd like to ask for Peace.
Yes, it's Peace I want,
And You, You won't deny the single wish of a child.
You created the Land of Peace,
Where stands the City of Peace,
Where stood the Temple of Peace,
But where still there is no Peace...
What shall I ask you for, God? I have everything.
Peace is what I ask for,
Only Peace.

(SHLOMIT GROSSBERG, AGE 13, JERUSALEM)

When will peace take over?
When will it come, the day?
When with armies and bombs will they
do away,
When all this hostility cease,
A day on which battleships
Will become palaces of leisure and fun
Floating on the seas.
A day on which the steel of guns
Will be melted into pleasure cars,
A day on which generals will begin to
raise flowers.
When peace
Will include all the peoples of these
neighboring lands,
When Ishmael and Israel
Will go hand in hand,

And when every Jew
The Arab's brother will be.
When will it come, the day?

(MAHMOUD ABU RADJ, AGE 12, KFAR SACHNIN, AN
ARAB VILLAGE IN THE GALILEE)

Wildpeace

Not the peace of a cease-fire
not even the vision of the wolf and the lamb,
but rather
as in the heart when the excitement is over
and you can talk only about a great weariness.
I know that I know how to kill,
that makes me an adult.
And my son plays with a toy gun that knows
how to open and close its eyes and say Mama.
A peace
without the big noise of beating swords into
ploughshares,
without words, without
the thud of the heavy rubber stamp: let it be
light, floating, like lazy white foam.
A little rest for the wounds—
who speaks of healing?
(And the howl of the orphans is passed from one
    generation
to the next, as in a relay race:
the baton never falls.)
Let it come
like wildflowers,

suddenly, because the field
must have it: wildpeace.

(YEHUDA AMICHAI)

Interfaith Prayers for Peace

O God, you are the source of life and peace.
Praised be your name forever.
We know it is you who turn our minds to thoughts of
peace.
Hear our prayer in this time of war.
Your power changes hearts.
Muslims, Christians, and Jews remember, and
profoundly affirm,
that they are followers of the one God,
children of Abraham, brothers and sisters.
Enemies begin to speak to one another;
those who were estranged join hands in friendship;
nations seek the way of peace together.
Strengthen our resolve to give witness to these
truths by the way we live.
Give to us:
understanding that puts an end to strife;
mercy that quenches hatred; and
forgiveness that overcomes vengeance.
Empower all people to live in your law of love.
Amen.

———————●———————

We pray for Israel,
Both the mystic ideal of our ancestors' dreams,
And the living miracle, here and now,
Built of heart, muscle, and steel.

May she endure and guard her soul,
Surviving the relentless, age-old hatreds,
The cynical concealment of diplomatic deceit,
And the rumblings that warn of war.
May Israel continue to be the temple that magnetizes
The loving eyes of Jews in all corners:
The Jew in a land of affluence and relative peace
Who forgets the glory and pain of his being,
And the Jew in a land of oppression whose bloodied fist
Beats in anguish and pride
Against the cage of his enslavement.
May Israel yet embrace her homeless, her own,
And bind the ingathered into one people.
May those who yearn for a society built on human
   concern
Find the vision of the prophets realized in her.
May her readiness to defend
Never diminish her search for peace.
May we always dare to hope
That in our day the antagonisms will end,
That all the displaced, Arab and Jew, will be rooted
   again,
That within Israel and across her borders
All God's children will touch hands in peace.

(NAHUM WALDMAN)

———————————●———————————

Eternal God, whose presence is over all of us, help us through
our prayers and our deeds to be able to build trust between us
and our enemies. We ask You to spread Your shelter of peace
over the State of Israel, granting safety to those who guard and
those who watch, giving skill to those who negotiate, so that

the peoples of Israel and Palestine may come to a closer understanding of each other. Help them to overcome prejudice and anger, hatred and fear, so that they may learn to live side by side in peace and harmony. May Your Divine Presence, Your light and Your love shine down upon these troubled souls, comforting the bereaved, healing and soothing all pain, enabling them to raise their spirits of hope and understanding, so that in our lifetime we shall be able to know how good and how pleasant it is for brothers and sisters to dwell together.

Hineih mah tov umah na-im   הִנֵּה מַה־טּוֹב וּמַה־נָּעִים

shevet achim gam yachad.   שֶׁבֶת אַחִים גַּם־יָחַד.

How good and how pleasant it is that siblings dwell together.

(PSALM 133:1)

עוֹד יָבוֹא שָׁלוֹם עָלֵינוּ, עוֹד יָבוֹא שָׁלוֹם עָלֵינוּ,
עוֹד יָבוֹא שָׁלוֹם עָלֵינוּ, וְעַל כֻּלָּם.
סָלָאם, עָלֵינוּ וְעַל כָּל הָעוֹלָם, סָלָאם, סָלָאם.

*Od yavo shalom aleinu, od yavo shalom aleinu, od yavo
shalom aleinu, v'al kulam.*
Salaam, aleinu v'al kol haolam, salaam, salaam.

Peace will surely come to us, to everyone.
Salaam, for us and for the entire world.

(MUSHE BEN-ARI)

6 PRAYERS UPON LEAVING ISRAEL

בָּרוּךְ אַתָּה, יְיָ אֱלֹהֵינוּ, מֶלֶךְ הָעוֹלָם, שֶׁעָזַר לָנוּ
לַעֲשׂוֹת נִסִּים לְעַצְמֵנוּ וּלְבָנֵינוּ בַּיָּמִים הָהֵם בַּזְּמַן
הַזֶּה. נַמְשִׁיךְ לַעֲשׂוֹת נִסִּים בְּיַחַד לִיצוֹר
מְדִינַת יִשְׂרָאֵל לְפִי דִּבְרֵי הַנְּבִיאִים, וְנֹאמַר:
לַשָּׁנָה הַבָּאָה בִּירוּשָׁלָיִם.

*Baruch atah, Adonai Eloheinu, Melech haolam, she-azar lanu
laasot nisim l'atzmeinu ul'vaneinu bayamim haheim baz'man
hazeh. Namshich laasot nisim b'yachad litzor M'dinat Yisrael
l'fi divrei han'vi-im, v'nomar: Lashanah habaah birushalayim.*

Praised are You, Adonai our God, Sovereign of the
universe, who helped us to make miracles for ourselves
and our children in ancient days. Let us continue to
make miracles together to fashion the State of Israel
according to the teachings of our prophets, and let us
say: Next year in Jerusalem!

———————————●———————————

Adonai our God and God of our ancestors, we offer You
grateful thanks for this good land that you gave to our ancestors.

As we depart, we pray for Israel's peace and prosperity, security and well-being.

May we merit seeing in our own lifetime the flowering of redemption and peace.

And may it be your will, Adonai our God, that we return here soon.

If I forget you, O Jerusalem,
May my right hand wither;
Let my tongue stick to my palate
If I cease to think of you,
If I do not keep Jerusalem in memory
Even at my happiest hour.

(PSALM 137:5)

7 PRAYERS UPON RETURNING HOME

May Adonai bless you from Zion;
May you share the prosperity of Jerusalem
All the days of your life,
And live to see your children's children.
May all be well with Israel!

(PSALM 128:5–6)

May the One who blessed our ancestors
Abraham, Isaac, and Jacob,
Sarah, Rebecca, Rachel, and Leah,
bless and make blessings of we who have traveled
to the Land of Israel
and have returned home in peace and well-being.
May the memories of our journey remain strong
and inspire us in our learning and in our deeds.
May the connections we have forged
to the Land of Israel and its people
remain a source of pride and inspiration.
May we work to build and maintain bridges
of knowledge and understanding, dialogue and support
between members of our congregation
and the people of the Land of Israel.
May we encourage others
to learn about and travel to the Land of Israel,
ancient birthplace of our faith and people,
and the modern homeland of Jewish hopes
and aspirations.

May we be blessed in the future
to journey again to the Land of Israel
and celebrate its accomplishments and vision,
and that we might in our own days
see the vision of the prophet come to pass:
"They shall dwell under their vine and fig tree,
and none shall make them afraid" (Micah 4:4).

Chapter 7

Blessings for the Seven Species of the Land of Israel

כִּי יְיָ אֱלֹהֶיךָ מְבִיאֲךָ אֶל־אֶרֶץ טוֹבָה, אֶרֶץ נַחֲלֵי
מַיִם עֲיָנֹת וּתְהֹמֹת יֹצְאִים בַּבִּקְעָה וּבָהָר. אֶרֶץ
חִטָּה וּשְׂעֹרָה וְגֶפֶן וּתְאֵנָה וְרִמּוֹן, אֶרֶץ־זֵית שֶׁמֶן
וּדְבָשׁ. אֶרֶץ אֲשֶׁר לֹא בְמִסְכֵּנֻת תֹּאכַל־בָּהּ לֶחֶם
לֹא־תֶחְסַר כֹּל בָּהּ, אֶרֶץ אֲשֶׁר אֲבָנֶיהָ בַרְזֶל
וּמֵהֲרָרֶיהָ תַּחְצֹב נְחֹשֶׁת. וְאָכַלְתָּ וְשָׂבָעְתָּ,
וּבֵרַכְתָּ אֶת־יְיָ אֱלֹהֶיךָ עַל־הָאָרֶץ הַטֹּבָה אֲשֶׁר
נָתַן לָךְ.

*Ki Adonai Elohecha m'viacha el eretz tovah, eretz nachalei
mayim ayanot ut'homot yotz'im babikah u'vahar. Eretz chitah
us'orah v'gefen ut'einah v'rimon, eretz zeit shemen ud'vash.
Eretz asher lo v'miskeinut tochal-bah lechem lo techsar kol
bah… V'achalta v'savata, u'veirachta et Adonai Elohecha al
haaretz hatovah asher natan lach.*

For Adonai your God is bringing you into a good land,
a land with streams and springs and fountains issuing
from plain and hill; a land of wheat and barley, of vines,
figs, and pomegranates, a land of olive trees and honey; a

land where you may eat food without stint.… When you
have eaten your fill, give thanks to Adonai your God for
the good land which God has given you.

(DEUTERONOMY 8:7–10)

For Fruit (grapes, figs, pomegranates, olives, and dates)

Baruch atah, Adonai Eloheinu,

Melech haolam,

borei p'ri ha-eitz.

בָּרוּךְ אַתָּה, יְיָ אֱלֹהֵינוּ,

מֶלֶךְ הָעוֹלָם,

בּוֹרֵא פְּרִי הָעֵץ.

Praised are You, Adonai our God, Sovereign of the
universe, who creates the fruit of the tree.

For Wine or Grape Juice

Baruch atah, Adonai Eloheinu,

Melech haolam,

borei p'ri hagafen.

בָּרוּךְ אַתָּה, יְיָ אֱלֹהֵינוּ,

מֶלֶךְ הָעוֹלָם,

בּוֹרֵא פְּרִי הַגָּפֶן.

Praised are You, Adonai our God, Sovereign of the
universe, who creates the fruit of the vine.

For Bread

Baruch atah, Adonai Eloheinu,

Melech haolam,

hamotzi lechem min haaretz.

בָּרוּךְ אַתָּה, יְיָ אֱלֹהֵינוּ,

מֶלֶךְ הָעוֹלָם,

הַמּוֹצִיא לֶחֶם מִן הָאָרֶץ.

Praised are You, Adonai our God, Sovereign of the
universe, who brings forth bread from the earth.

Birkat HaMazon: Blessing after Eating— Short Form

On Shabbat and Holidays

Shir hamaalot, b'shuv Adonai	שִׁיר הַמַּעֲלוֹת, בְּשׁוּב יְיָ
et shivat Tziyon, hayinu k'cholmim.	אֶת־שִׁיבַת צִיּוֹן, הָיִינוּ כְּחֹלְמִים.
Az yimalei s'chok, pinu	אָז יִמָּלֵא שְׂחוֹק פִּינוּ
ul'shoneinu rinah.	וּלְשׁוֹנֵנוּ רִנָּה.
Az yomru vagoyim,	אָז יֹאמְרוּ בַגּוֹיִם,
higdil Adonai laasot im eileh.	הִגְדִּיל יְיָ לַעֲשׂוֹת עִם־אֵלֶּה.
Higdil Adonai laasot imanu,	הִגְדִּיל יְיָ לַעֲשׂוֹת עִמָּנוּ,
hayinu s'meichim.	הָיִינוּ שְׂמֵחִים.
Shuvah Adonai et sh'viteinu	שׁוּבָה יְיָ אֶת־שְׁבִיתֵנוּ
kaafikim banegev.	כַּאֲפִיקִים בַּנֶּגֶב.
Hazorim b'dimah b'rinah yiktzoru.	הַזֹּרְעִים בְּדִמְעָה בְּרִנָּה יִקְצֹרוּ.
Haloch yeileich uvachoh	הָלוֹךְ יֵלֵךְ וּבָכֹה
nosei meshech hazarah,	נֹשֵׂא מֶשֶׁךְ־הַזָּרַע,
bo yavo v'rinah, nosei alumotav.	בֹּא־יָבוֹא בְרִנָּה נֹשֵׂא אֲלֻמֹּתָיו.

A song of ascents. When Adonai restores the fortunes of Zion, we see it as in a dream, our mouths shall be filled with laughter, our tongues, with songs of joy. Then shall they say among the nations, "Adonai has done great things for them!" Adonai will do great things for us and we shall rejoice. Restore our fortunes, Adonai, like watercourses in the Negev. They who sow in tears shall reap with songs of joy. Those who go forth weeping, carrying the seed-bag, shall come back with songs of joy, carrying their sheaves.

All Days

Leader

Chaveirim vachaveirot, n'vareich!

חֲבֵרִים וַחֲבֵרוֹת, נְבָרֵךְ!

Let us praise God.

Group

Y'hi shem Adonai m'vorach

mei-atah v'ad olam.

יְהִי שֵׁם יְיָ מְבֹרָךְ

מֵעַתָּה וְעַד עוֹלָם.

Praised be the name of God, now and forever!

Leader

Y'hi shem Adonai m'vorach

mei-atah v'ad olam.

Bir'shut hachevrah, n'vareich Eloheinu

she-achalnu mishelo.

יְהִי שֵׁם יְיָ מְבֹרָךְ

מֵעַתָּה וְעַד עוֹלָם.

בִּרְשׁוּת הַחֶבְרָה, נְבָרֵךְ אֱלֹהֵינוּ

שֶׁאָכַלְנוּ מִשֶּׁלוֹ.

Praised be the name of God, now and forever!
Praised be our God, of whose abundance we have eaten.

Group

Baruch Eloheinu she-achalnu

mishelo uv'tuvo chayinu.

בָּרוּךְ אֱלֹהֵינוּ שֶׁאָכַלְנוּ

מִשֶּׁלוֹ וּבְטוּבוֹ חָיִינוּ.

Praised be our God, of whose abundance we have eaten,
and by whose goodness we live.

Leader

Baruch Eloheinu she-achalnu

mishelo uv'tuvo chayinu.

Baruch hu uvaruch sh'mo.

בָּרוּךְ אֱלֹהֵינוּ שֶׁאָכַלְנוּ

מִשֶּׁלוֹ וּבְטוּבוֹ חָיִינוּ.

בָּרוּךְ הוּא וּבָרוּךְ שְׁמוֹ.

Praised be our God, of whose abundance we have eaten,
and by whose goodness we live.
Praised be God and praised be God's name.

Group

Baruch atah, Adonai Eloheinu,	בָּרוּךְ אַתָּה, יְיָ אֱלֹהֵינוּ,
Melech haolom, hazan et haolam	מֶלֶךְ הָעוֹלָם, הַזָּן אֶת־הָעוֹלָם
kulo b'tuvo, b'chein b'chesed	כֻּלּוֹ בְּטוּבוֹ, בְּחֵן בְּחֶסֶד
uv'rachamim.	וּבְרַחֲמִים.
Hu notein lechem l'chol basar,	הוּא נוֹתֵן לֶחֶם לְכָל־בָּשָׂר,
ki l'olam chasdo.	כִּי לְעוֹלָם חַסְדּוֹ.
Uv'tuvo hagadol tamid lo chasar lanu,	וּבְטוּבוֹ הַגָּדוֹל תָּמִיד לֹא חָסַר לָנוּ,
v'al yechsar lanu mazon l'olam va-ed.	וְאַל יֶחְסַר לָנוּ מָזוֹן לְעוֹלָם וָעֶד.
Baavur sh'mo hagadol,	בַּעֲבוּר שְׁמוֹ הַגָּדוֹל,
ki hu El zan um'farneis lakol,	כִּי הוּא אֵל זָן וּמְפַרְנֵס לַכֹּל,
umeitiv lakol, umeichin mazon	וּמֵטִיב לַכֹּל, וּמֵכִין מָזוֹן
l'chol b'riyotav asher bara.	לְכָל בְּרִיּוֹתָיו אֲשֶׁר בָּרָא.
Baruch atah, Adonai, hazan et hakol.	בָּרוּךְ אַתָּה, יְיָ, הַזָּן אֶת־הַכֹּל.

Sovereign God of the universe, we praise You: Your
goodness sustains the world.
You are the God of grace, love, and compassion, the
Source of bread for all who live;
for Your love is everlasting. In Your great goodness we
need never lack for food;
You provide food enough for all. We praise You, O God,
Source of food for all who live.

Kakatuv, v'achalta v'savata,	כַּכָּתוּב: וְאָכַלְתָּ וְשָׂבָעְתָּ,
uveirachta et Adonai Elohecha	וּבֵרַכְתָּ אֶת־יְיָ אֱלֹהֶיךָ

al haaretz hatovah asher natan lach.   עַל הָאָרֶץ הַטּוֹבָה אֲשֶׁר נָתַן לָךְ.

Baruch atah, Adonai,   בָּרוּךְ אַתָּה, יְיָ,

al haaretz v'al hamazon.   עַל הָאָרֶץ וְעַל הַמָּזוֹן.

As it is written: "When you have eaten and are satisfied,
give praise to your God who has given you this good
earth."
We praise You, O God, for the earth and for its
sustenance.

Uv'neih Y'rushalayim ir hakodesh   וּבְנֵה יְרוּשָׁלַיִם עִיר הַקֹּדֶשׁ

bimheirah v'yameinu.   בִּמְהֵרָה בְיָמֵינוּ.

Baruch atah, Adonai,   בָּרוּךְ אַתָּה, יְיָ,

boneh v'rachamav Y'rushalayim. Amen.   בּוֹנֶה בְרַחֲמָיו יְרוּשָׁלַיִם, אָמֵן.

Let Jerusalem, the holy city, be renewed in our time.
We praise You, Adonai, in compassion You rebuild
Jerusalem. Amen.

Harachaman, hu yimloch   הָרַחֲמָן, הוּא יִמְלוֹךְ

aleinu l'olam va-ed.   עָלֵינוּ לְעוֹלָם וָעֶד.

Merciful One, be our God for ever.

Harachaman, hu yitbarach   הָרַחֲמָן, הוּא יִתְבָּרַךְ

bashamayim u'vaaretz.   בַּשָּׁמַיִם וּבָאָרֶץ.

Merciful One, heaven and earth alike are blessed
by Your presence.

Harachaman, hu yishlach b'rachah   הָרַחֲמָן, הוּא יִשְׁלַח בְּרָכָה

m'rubah   מְרֻבָּה

babayit hazeh,   בַּבַּיִת הַזֶּה,

v'al shulchan zeh she-achalnu alav. וְעַל שֻׁלְחָן זֶה שֶׁאָכַלְנוּ עָלָיו.

Merciful One, bless this house and this table at
which we have eaten.

Harachaman, hu y'vareich הָרַחֲמָן, הוּא יְבָרֵךְ
et M'dinat Yisrael, אֶת מְדִינַת יִשְׂרָאֵל
reishit tz'michat g'ulateinu. רֵאשִׁית צְמִיחַת גְּאֻלָתֵנוּ.

Merciful One, bless the State of Israel, which marks the
dawning of hope for all who seek peace.

On Shabbat

Harachaman, hu yishlach lanu הָרַחֲמָן, הוּא יִשְׁלַח לָנוּ
et Eiliyahu HaNavi, zachur latov, אֶת אֵלִיָּהוּ הַנָּבִיא, זָכוּר לַטּוֹב,
vivaser lanu b'sorot tovot, וִיבַשֶּׂר־לָנוּ בְּשׂוֹרוֹת טוֹבוֹת,
y'shuot v'nechamot. יְשׁוּעוֹת וְנֶחָמוֹת.

Merciful One, send us tidings of Elijah,
glimpses of good to come,
redemption and consolation.

Harachaman, hu yanchileinu הָרַחֲמָן, הוּא יַנְחִילֵנוּ
yom shekulo Shabbat um'nuchah l'chayei יוֹם שֶׁכֻּלּוֹ שַׁבָּת וּמְנוּחָה לְחַיֵּי
haolamim. הָעוֹלָמִים.

Merciful One, help us to see the coming of a time
when all is Shabbat.

On Yom Tov

Harachaman, hu yanchileinu הָרַחֲמָן, הוּא יַנְחִילֵנוּ
yom shekulo tov. יוֹם שֶׁכֻּלּוֹ טוֹב.

Merciful One, help us to see the coming of a time
when all is good.

All Days

Oseh shalom bimromav,	עֹשֶׂה שָׁלוֹם בִּמְרוֹמָיו,
hu yaaseh shalom,	הוּא יַעֲשֶׂה שָׁלוֹם
aleinu v'al kol Yisrael,	עָלֵינוּ וְעַל כָּל יִשְׂרָאֵל,
v'al kol yosh'vei teiveil, v'imru amen.	וְעַל כָּל יוֹשְׁבֵי תֵבֵל, וְאִמְרוּ אָמֵן.

May the Source of peace grant peace
to us, to all Israel, and to all the world.

Adonai oz l'amo yitein.	יְיָ עֹז לְעַמּוֹ יִתֵּן.
Adonai y'vareich et amo vashalom.	יְיָ יְבָרֵךְ אֶת־עַמּוֹ בַשָּׁלוֹם.

May Adonai grant strength to our people.
May Adonai bless our people with peace.

9 HAVDALAH

As Shabbat ends, the Havdalah candle is lit.

הִנֵּה אֵל יְשׁוּעָתִי, אֶבְטַח וְלֹא אֶפְחָד.

כִּי עָזִּי וְזִמְרָת יָהּ יְיָ, וַיְהִי לִי לִישׁוּעָה.

וּשְׁאַבְתֶּם מַיִם בְּשָׂשׂוֹן מִמַּעַיְנֵי הַיְשׁוּעָה.

לַיְיָ הַיְשׁוּעָה, עַל עַמְּךָ בִרְכָתֶךָ, סֶּלָה.

יְיָ צְבָאוֹת עִמָּנוּ, מִשְׂגָּב לָנוּ אֱלֹהֵי יַעֲקֹב סֶלָה.

יְיָ צְבָאוֹת, אַשְׁרֵי אָדָם בֹּטֵחַ בָּךְ.

יְיָ הוֹשִׁיעָה, הַמֶּלֶךְ יַעֲנֵנוּ בְיוֹם קָרְאֵנוּ.

לַיְהוּדִים הָיְתָה אוֹרָה וְשִׂמְחָה וְשָׂשׂוֹן וִיקָר;

כֵּן תִּהְיֶה לָנוּ. כּוֹס יְשׁוּעוֹת אֶשָּׂא, וּבְשֵׁם יְיָ
אֶקְרָא.

Hineih El y'shuati, evtach v'lo efchad.
Ki ozi v'zimrat Yah Adonai, vay'hi li lishuah.
Ush'avtem mayim b'sason mima-ainei hay'shuah.
L'Adonai hay'shuah, al amcha virchatecha, selah.
Adonai tz'vaot imanu, misgav lanu Elohei Yaakov, selah.
Adonai tz'vaot, ashrei adam botei-ach bach.
Adonai hoshiah, haMelech yaaneinu v'yom koreinu.
La-Y'hudim hay'tah orah v'simchah v'sason vikar;
kein tih'yeh lanu. Kos y'shuot esa, uv'sheim Adonai ekra.

Behold the God who gives me triumph! I am confident, unafraid; for Adonai is my strength and might, and has been my deliverance. Joyfully shall you draw water from the fountains of triumph, deliverance is Adonai's; Your blessing be upon Your people! *Selah*.

Adonai Tz'vaot is with us; the God of Jacob is our haven. *Selah*.

Adonai Tz'vaot, happy is the one who trusts in You.

O Adonai, grant victory!

May the Sovereign answer us when we call.

The Jews enjoyed light and gladness, happiness and honor. So may it be for us.

I raise the cup of deliverance and invoke the name of Adonai.

The Wine or Grape Juice

The blessing may be said over wine or grape juice.

Lift the goblet but do not drink until after the Blessing of Separation.

Baruch atah, Adonai	בָּרוּךְ אַתָּה, יְיָ
Eloheinu, Melech haolam,	אֱלֹהֵינוּ, מֶלֶךְ הָעוֹלָם,
borei p'ri hagafen.	בּוֹרֵא פְּרִי הַגָּפֶן.

Praise to You, Adonai our God, Sovereign of the universe, Creator of the fruit of the vine.

The Spices

Lift the spice box.

Baruch atah, Adonai	בָּרוּךְ אַתָּה, יְיָ
Eloheinu, Melech haolam,	אֱלֹהֵינוּ, מֶלֶךְ הָעוֹלָם,
borei minei v'samim.	בּוֹרֵא מִינֵי בְשָׂמִים.

Praise to You, Adonai our God, Sovereign of the universe, Creator of varied spices.

Circulate the spice box and smell the contents.

The Light

Raise the Havdalah candle.

Baruch atah, Adonai	בָּרוּךְ אַתָּה, יְיָ
Eloheinu, Melech haolam,	אֱלֹהֵינוּ, מֶלֶךְ הָעוֹלָם,
borei m'orei ha-eish.	בּוֹרֵא מְאוֹרֵי הָאֵשׁ.

Praise to You, Adonai our God, Sovereign of the universe, Creator of the lights of fire.

The Blessing of Separation

Baruch atah, Adonai	בָּרוּךְ אַתָּה, יְיָ
Eloheinu, Melech haolam,	אֱלֹהֵינוּ, מֶלֶךְ הָעוֹלָם,
hamavdil bein kodesh l'chol,	הַמַּבְדִּיל בֵּין קֹדֶשׁ לְחוֹל,
bein or l'choshech,	בֵּין אוֹר לְחֹשֶׁךְ,
bein Yisrael laamim,	בֵּין יִשְׂרָאֵל לָעַמִּים,
bein yom hashvi-i	בֵּין יוֹם הַשְּׁבִיעִי
l'sheishet y'mei hamaaseh.	לְשֵׁשֶׁת יְמֵי הַמַּעֲשֶׂה.
Baruch atah, Adonai,	בָּרוּךְ אַתָּה, יְיָ,
hamavdil bein kodesh l'chol.	הַמַּבְדִּיל בֵּין קֹדֶשׁ לְחוֹל.

Praise to You, Adonai our God, Sovereign of the universe:
who distinguishes between the holy and ordinary,
between light and dark,
between Israel and the nations, between the seventh day and the six days of work.

Praise to You, Adonai who distinguishes between the holy and ordinary.

Sip the wine or grape juice.

Extinguish the Havdalah candle in the remaining wine or grape juice, while the following passages are sung or said:

Hamavdil bein kodesh l'chol,	הַמַּבְדִּיל בֵּין קֹדֶשׁ לְחוֹל,
chatoteinu hu yimchol,	חַטֹּאתֵינוּ הוּא יִמְחֹל,
zareinu shlomeinu yarbeh kachol,	זַרְעֵנוּ שְׁלוֹמֵנוּ יַרְבֶּה כַחוֹל,
v'chakochavim balailah.	וְכַכּוֹכָבִים בַּלָּיְלָה.
Shavua tov...	שָׁבוּעַ טוֹב ...

May the One who distinguishes between the holy and the ordinary, pardon our sins; multiply our offspring and our peace as grains of sand and as the stars at night. A good week, a week of peace, may gladness reign and joy increase.

Eliyahu hanavi,	אֵלִיָּהוּ הַנָּבִיא,
Eliyahu hatishbi,	אֵלִיָּהוּ הַתִּשְׁבִּי,
Eliyahu hagiladi.	אֵלִיָּהוּ הַגִּלְעָדִי.
Bimheirah b'yameinu,	בִּמְהֵרָה בְיָמֵינוּ,
yavo eileinu,	יָבוֹא אֵלֵינוּ,
im Mashiach ben David.	עִם מָשִׁיחַ בֶּן־דָּוִד.

May Elijah the prophet,
Elijah the Tishbite,
Elijah of Gilead,
quickly in our day come to us
heralding redemption.

10 SONGS OF ISRAEL

HaTikvah

Kol od balevav p'nimah

nefesh Y'hudi homiyah

ul'faatei mizrach kadimah

ayin l'Tzion tzofiyah.

Od lo avdah tikvateinu

hatikvah bat sh'not alpayim

lih'yot am chofshi b'artzeinu,

Eretz Tziyon viY'rushalayim.

כָּל עוֹד בַּלֵּבָב פְּנִימָה

נֶפֶשׁ יְהוּדִי הוֹמִיָּה.

וּלְפַאֲתֵי מִזְרָח קָדִימָה

עַיִן לְצִיּוֹן צוֹפִיָּה.

עוֹד לֹא אָבְדָה תִּקְוָתֵנוּ,

הַתִּקְוָה בַּת שְׁנוֹת אַלְפַּיִם,

לִהְיוֹת עַם חָפְשִׁי בְּאַרְצֵנוּ,

אֶרֶץ צִיּוֹן וִירוּשָׁלָיִם.

So long as within the inmost heart a Jewish spirit sings,
so long as the eye looks eastward, gazing toward Zion,
our hope is not lost—the hope of two thousand years:
to be a free people in our land, the land of Zion and
Jerusalem.

(NAFTALI HERZ IMBER)

Y'rushalayim (Mei-Al Pisgat Har Hatzofim)

Mei-al pisgat Har Hatzofim,

shalom lach Y'rushalayim!

Mei-al pisgat Har Hatzofim,

eshtachaveh lach apayim.

מֵעַל פִּסְגַּת הַר הַצּוֹפִים,

שָׁלוֹם לָךְ יְרוּשָׁלָיִם.

מֵעַל פִּסְגַּת הַר הַצּוֹפִים,

אֶשְׁתַּחֲוֶה לָךְ אַפָּיִם.

	מֵאָה דּוֹרוֹת
Mei-ah dorot	
chalamti alayich,	חָלַמְתִּי עָלַיִךְ,
lizkot lirot b'or panayich.	לִזְכּוֹת לִרְאוֹת בְּאוֹר פָּנָיִךְ.
Y'rushalayim, Y'rushalayim!	יְרוּשָׁלַיִם, יְרוּשָׁלַיִם!
Ha-iri panayich livneich!	הָאִירִי פָּנַיִךְ לִבְנֵךְ!
Y'rushalayim, Y'rushalayim!	יְרוּשָׁלַיִם, יְרוּשָׁלַיִם!
Meichorvotayich evneich.	מֵחָרְבוֹתַיִךְ אֶבְנֵךְ!

From the peak of Mount Scopus, "Shalom," Jerusalem!
From the peak of Mount Scopus, I bow down low before
you. A hundred generations I have dreamed of you,
dreamed of the privilege to bask in light. Jerusalem,
Jerusalem! Smile on your children! Jerusalem,
Jerusalem! Out of your ruins will I rebuild you!

(Avigdor Hameiri)

Y'rushalayim Shel Zahav (Jerusalem of Gold)

אֲוִיר הָרִים צָלוּל כַּיַּיִן וְרֵיחַ אֳרָנִים
נִשָּׂא בְּרוּחַ הָעַרְבַּיִם עִם קוֹל פַּעֲמוֹנִים.

Avir harim tzalul kayayin v'rei-ach oranim
nisa b'ruach haarbayim im kol paamonim.

וּבְתַרְדֵּמַת אִילָן וָאֶבֶן שְׁבוּיָה בַּחֲלוֹמָהּ
הָעִיר אֲשֶׁר בָּדָד יוֹשֶׁבֶת וּבְלִבָּהּ חוֹמָה.

יְרוּשָׁלַיִם שֶׁל זָהָב
וְשֶׁל נְחֹשֶׁת וְשֶׁל אוֹר

הֲלֹא לְכָל שִׁירַיִךְ אֲנִי כִּנּוֹר!

אֵיכָה יָבְשׁוּ בּוֹרוֹת הַמַּיִם,

כִּכָּר הַשּׁוּק רֵיקָה.

וְאֵין פּוֹקֵד אֶת הַר הַבַּיִת

בָּעִיר הָעַתִּיקָה.

Uv'tardeimat ilan va-even sh'vuyah bachalomah
ha-ir asher badad yoshevet uv'libah chomah.

Y'rushalayim shel zahav
v'shel n'choshet v'shel or
Halo l'chol shirayich ani kinor!

Eichah yav'shu borot hamayim,
kikar hashuk reikah.
V'ein pokeid et Har Habayit
ba-Ir Haatikah.

וּבַמְּעָרוֹת אֲשֶׁר בַּסֶּלַע

מְיַלְּלוֹת רוּחוֹת.

וְאֵין יוֹרֵד אֶל יַם הַמֶּלַח

בְּדֶרֶךְ יְרִיחוֹ.

אַךְ בְּבוֹאִי הַיּוֹם לָשִׁיר לָךְ

וְלָךְ לִקְשֹׁר כְּתָרִים,

קָטֹנְתִּי מִצְּעִיר בָּנַיִךְ

וּמֵאַחֲרוֹן הַמְשׁוֹרְרִים.

Uvamarot asher basela
m'yal'lot ruchot.
V'ein yoreid el Yam Hamelach
b'derech Y'richo.

Ach b'vo-i hayom lashir lach
v'lach likshor k'tarim,
katonti mitz'ir banayich
umei-acharon ham'shor'rim.

כִּי שְׁמֵךְ צוֹרֵב אֶת הַשְּׂפָתַיִם
כִּנְשִׁיקַת שָׂרָף.
אִם אֶשְׁכָּחֵךְ יְרוּשָׁלַיִם אֲשֶׁר כֻּלָּהּ זָהָב.

Ki sh'meich tzoreiv et has'fatayim
kin'shikat saraf.
Im eshkacheich Y'rushalayim asher kulah zahav.

חָזַרְנוּ אֶל בּוֹרוֹת הַמַּיִם לַשּׁוּק וְלַכִּכָּר
שׁוֹפָר קוֹרֵא בְּהַר הַבַּיִת בָּעִיר הָעַתִּיקָה.
וּבַמְּעָרוֹת אֲשֶׁר בַּסֶּלַע
אַלְפֵי שְׁמָשׁוֹת זוֹרְחוֹת
וְשׁוּב נֵרֵד אֶל יַם הַמֶּלַח
בְּדֶרֶךְ יְרִיחוֹ.

Chazarnu el borot hamayim lashuk v'lakikar
shofar korei b'Har Habayit ba-Ir Haatikah.
Uvamarot asher basela
alfei sh'mashot zorchot
v'shuv neireid el Yam Hamelach
b'derech Y'richo.

The mountain air is clear as wine and the fragrance of
pine is carried in the evening breeze with the sound of
bells. In the slumber of tree and stone, captive within her
dream, is the city which sits deserted, and the wall at its
heart.

Jerusalem of gold, of bronze, and of light, am I not a
harp for all your songs?
How the cisterns have dried up! The market square is
empty. No one attends the Temple Mount in the Old
City. And in the caves in the rock winds moan. No one
descends to the Dead Sea by way of Jericho.

But when I come today to sing unto you and to bind
crowns for you, I become smaller than the youngest of
your sons or the least of the poets. For your name burns
the lips like the kiss of a seraph if I forget you,
O Jerusalem, that is all of gold.

We have returned to the cisterns, to the market and to
the square. A shofar calls out on the Temple Mount in
the Old City. And in the caves in the rock, thousands of
suns shine. We will once again descend to the Dead Sea
by way of Jericho.

Shir LaShalom

תְּנוּ לַשֶּׁמֶשׁ לַעֲלוֹת לַבֹּקֶר לְהָאִיר,
הַזַּכָּה שֶׁבַּתְּפִלּוֹת אוֹתָנוּ לֹא תַּחֲזִיר.
מִי אֲשֶׁר כָּבָה נֵרוֹ וּבֶעָפָר נִטְמָן,
בִּכְבִי מַר לֹא יָעִירוֹ לֹא יַחֲזִירוֹ לְכָאן.

אִישׁ אוֹתָנוּ לֹא יָשִׁיב

מִבּוֹר תַּחְתִּית אָפֵל, כָּאן לֹא יוֹעִילוּ

לֹא שִׂמְחַת הַנִּצָּחוֹן וְלֹא שִׁירֵי הַלֵּל.

לָכֵן רַק שִׁירוּ, שִׁיר לַשָּׁלוֹם

אַל תִּלְחֲשׁוּ תְּפִלָּה

מוּטָב תָּשִׁירוּ, שִׁיר לַשָּׁלוֹם

בִּצְעָקָה גְדוֹלָה.

תְּנוּ לַשֶּׁמֶשׁ לַחֲדֹר מִבַּעַד לַפְּרָחִים.

אַל תַּבִּיטוּ לְאָחוֹר, הַנִּיחוּ לַהוֹלְכִים.

שְׂאוּ עֵינַיִם בְּתִקְוָה, לֹא דֶּרֶךְ כַּוָּנוֹת

שִׁירוּ שִׁיר לָאַהֲבָה, וְלֹא לַמִּלְחָמוֹת.

אַל תַּגִּידוּ יוֹם יָבוֹא, הָבִיאוּ אֶת הַיּוֹם!

כִּי לֹא חֲלוֹם הוּא

וּבְכָל הַכִּכָּרוֹת הָרִיעוּ לַשָּׁלוֹם!

T'nu lashemesh laalot laboker l'ha-ir,
Hazakah shebat'filot otanu lo tachazir.
Mi asher kavah neiro uve-afar nitman,
bechi mar lo ya-iro lo yachaziro l'chan.

Ish otanu lo yashiv
mibor tachtit afoil, kan lo yo-ilu
lo simchat hanitzachon v'lo shirei haleil.

Lachein rak shiru, shir lashalom
al tilchashu t'filah

mutav tashiru, shir lashalom
bitz'akah g'dolah.

T'nu lashemesh lachador mibaad laprachim
al tabitu l'achor, hanichu laholchim.
S'u einayim b'tikvah, lo derech kavanot
shiru shir laahavah, v'lo lamilchamot.

Al tagidu yom yavo, haviu et hayom!
Ki lo chalom hu
uv'chol hakikarot hariu lashalom!

Let the sun rise, the morning dawn. The purest of prayers will not bring us back. Bitter crying will not awaken or return those whose candle has gone out and who have been buried in the dust. It won't return anyone to us from dark pits. Here neither joy of victory nor songs of praise will be of any use.

So just sing, sing for peace! Don't whisper a prayer. It is far better to sing for peace,
in one great shout.

Let the sun shine through the flowers. Don't look back; leave that to pedestrians. Lift up your eyes in hope, not through gun sights. Sing a song of love, not of war! Don't say the day will come. Bring the day! Because it is not a dream. In every city square cry out for peace.

(YAAKOV ROTBLIT AND MOSHE BEN-ARI)

Afterword

By the rivers of Babylon,
there we sat and wept
when we remembered Zion.
On the willows we hung our lyres.
There our captors demanded songs of us,
that our lyres should play joyful music.
"Sing for us from Zion's song."
How can we sing the song of Adonai on alien soil?
If I forget you, O Jerusalem,
let my right hand wither.
May my tongue cleave to my palate
if I fail to remember you,
If I fail to elevate Jerusalem above my highest joy.

(PSALM 137:1–6)

Finding a Reform Congregation in Israel

Israel Movement for Reform and
Progressive Judaism
http://www.reform.org.il/eng/
13 King David Street,
Jerusalem 94101, Israel
Telephone: 02–6203448
Fax: 02–6203446
E-mail: info@impj.org.il

Jerusalem & Area

Kehilat Har-El
www.kharel.org.il

Kehilat Kol HaNeshama
www.kolhaneshama.org.il

Kehilat Mevakshei Derech
http://mevakshei.org

K'hillat M'vassert Tzion (KaMaTz)
www.kamatz.org

Kehillat Tzur Hadassah
www.kbyonline.org/tzurhadassah/

North

Kehilat Har Halutz
http://www.halutz.org.il

Kehilat Sulam Yaakov (Zichron
Yaakov)
www.facebook.com/K.Sulam.Yaakov

Kehilat Ohel Avraham (Haifa)
http://www.leobaeck.org.il/english/

Kehilat Or Hadash (Haifa)
www.or-hadash-haifa.org

Kehilat Shirat HaYam B'Karmel
(Haifa)
www.shirathayamcarmel.org.il

Kehilat Ma'alot Tiv'on (Kiryat Tivon)
www.maalotivon.com

Kehilat Yedid Nefesh (Karmiel)
www.yedidnefesh.co.il

Kehilat Emet v'Shalom (Nahariyah)
www.2all.co.il/Web/Sites/pjn

Central

Kehilat HaShachar (Even Yehuda)
http://kehilat-hashachar-even-
yehuda.blogspot.com/

Kehilat Sha'are Kedem (Herzliya)
www.shaare-kedem.org.il

Kehilat Kodesh veChol (Holon)
www.kholon.org

Kehilat YoZMA (Modi'in)
www.yozma.org.il

Kehilat Natan-Yah (Netanyah)
www.natan-ya.org

Kehilat Birkat Shalom (Kibbutz
Gezer)
www.birkatshalom.net

Kehilat Brit Olam (Kiryat Ono)
www.britolamono.org.il

Kehilat Bavat Ayin (Rosh Ha'Ayin)
www.bavat-ayin.org.il

Kehilat Achvat Yisrael (Rishon
L'Tziyon)
www.achvatisrael.org.il

Kehilat Darchei Noam (Ramat
HaSharon)
www.d-noam.org

Kehilat Ranana (Ranana)
www.raanan.org

Kehilat Beit Daniel (Tel Aviv)
www.beit-daniel.org.il

Sources

Every effort has been made to ascertain the owners of copyrights for the selections used in this volume and to obtain permission to reprint copyrighted passages. The Central Conference of American Rabbis will be pleased, in subsequent editions, to correct any inadvertent errors or omissions that may be pointed out.

In addition to the specific acknowledgments listed below, the CCAR extends its thanks to the University Press of Nebraska for permission to adapt selected Psalm and Biblical texts from the *JPS Tanakh: The Holy Scriptures,* © 1985 by The Jewish Publication Society, Philadelphia.

1. Prayers before Leaving for Israel

5 "May God who called our ancestors," adapted from *Forms of Prayer for Jewish Worship* © 1977 by Reform Synagogues of Great Britain, p. 292.

6 "God within and beyond me," by Serge Lippe

7 *Mi Shebeirach* on Behalf of One Traveling to Israel, adapted from *Kol HaNeshamah: Shabbat Vehagim* © 1994 by The Reconstructionist Press, p. 693, 101 Greenwood Ave., Ste. 430, Jenkintown, PA 19046. Fax: 215–885–5603, Phone: 877–JRF-PUBS, Email: press@jrf.org, Website: www.jrfbookstore.com; and from *Moreh Derekh: The Rabbi's Manual of the Rabbinical Assembly,* edited by Perry Raphael Rank and Gordon M. Freeman © 1998 by the Rabbinical Assembly, p. L-7.

7 *Mi Shebeirach* Recited by the Traveler to Israel, adapted from *Kol HaNeshamah: Shabbat Vehagim* © 1994 by The Reconstructionist Press, p. 693.

8 *T'filat HaDerech,* from *Mishkan T'filah: A Reform Siddur* © 2007 by the Central Conference of American Rabbis, p. 378.

9 *T'filat HaDerech,* by Debbie Friedman © by the Estate of Debbie Friedman.

10 For a Trip to Israel, adapted from Psalm 122 in *JPS Tanakh* © 1985, 1999 by The Jewish Publication Society, Philadelphia. Reprinted with permission of the University of Nebraska Press.

10 "Behold I am about to fulfill the mitzvah," adapted from *Moreh Derekh: The Rabbi's Manual of the Rabbinical Assembly,* edited by Perry Raphael Rank and Gordon M. Freeman © 1998 by the Rabbinical Assembly.

11 *L'chi Lach,* by Debbie Friedman © by the Estate of Debbie Friedman.

11 "God… I am returning once again," adapted from *Moreh Derekh: The Rabbi's Manual of the Rabbinical Assembly*, edited by Perry Raphael Rank and Gordon M. Freeman © 1998 by the Rabbinical Assembly.

2. Prayers upon Arriving in Israel

14 "On this soil sacred to memory," adapted from *On the Doorposts of Your House*, Revised Edition © 1994, 2007 by the Central Conference of American Rabbis, p. 160.

15 "This whole land belongs," from "Gazelle I Send You (1972)" by Amir Gilboa, in *Israeli Poetry: A Contemporary Anthology*, selected and translated by Warren Bargad and Stanley F. Chyet © 1986 by the Indiana University Press, pp. 30–31. Used by permission.

15 "My heart, homeland," by Esther Raab © 2002, Harold Schimmel, appeared first in *Thistles: Selected Poems of Esther Raab*, translated by Harold Schimmel, published by Ibis Editions, Jerusalem, p. 41.

3. Prayers and Readings for Visiting Special Sites

16 "From Atop Mount Scopus," by Avigdor Hameiri, © Acum Ltd.

17 *Y'rushalayim Shel Zahav*, text by Naomi Shemer © Acum, Ltd. Translation from *Mishkan T'filah: A Reform Siddur*, © 2007 by the Central Conference of American Rabbis, p. 661.

17 "We pray to stand upright," adapted from *G'vurot* for Yom Kippur in *Gates of Repentance: The New Union Prayerbook for the Days of Awe* © 1978, 1996 by the Central Conference of American Rabbis, p. 400.

18 "One does not travel to Jerusalem," by Yitzhak Yasinowitz, translated from Yiddish by Miriam Grossman in *Yom Kippur Readings*, edited by Rabbi Dov Peretz Elkins © 2005 by Jewish Lights Publishing.

18 "The Land of Israel by Foot," by Amos Keinan, translated by Josh Weinberg.

19 Psalm 126, translation adapted from *JPS Tanakh* © 1985, 1999 by The Jewish Publication Society, Philadelphia. Reprinted with permission of the University of Nebraska Press.

19 "Eternal God… show compassion for Israel," from the full *Birkat HaMazon*.

20 "Who'd have dared shaped the thought?" from "Jerusalem, June 1967" by Stanley F. Chyet. Reprinted with the permission of the Chyet family.

21 "There Are Hearts, There Are Hearts," by Julie Silver © 1992 Sliver Girl Music (ASCAP), based on the Hebrew from a speech by Rabbi

Abraham Isaac Kook. Used by permission.

21 "This Wall has heard many prayers," from "The Paratroopers Cry" by Chaim Hefer, translated by Michael Graetz.

22 "The Wall," by Abraham Joshua Heschel, in *Israel: An Echo of Eternity* © 1967, 1968, 1969 by Abraham Joshua Heschel, Farrar, Straus and Giroux, p. 19.

22 "Tzelofhad's Daughters," by Abby Caplin © 2010 by Abby Caplin. All rights reserved.

23 Lamentations 2:10–13, from *JPS Tanakh* © 1985, 1999 by The Jewish Publication Society, Philadelphia. Reprinted by permission of the University of Nebraska Press.

24 "Yizkor... we remember," by Peter Knobel, in *Mishkan T'filah: A Reform Siddur* © 2007 by the Central Conference of American Rabbis, p. 534.

25 "El malei rachamim," translated by Kinneret Shiryon, in *Mishkan T'filah: A Reform Siddur* © 2007 by the Central Conference of American Rabbis, p. 536.

26 "Standing here at the graves," by Serge Lippe.

27 "Blessed is the match," by Hannah Senesh, in *Hannah Senesh: Her Life and Diary*, translated by Marie Syrkin.

27 "There are stars up above," by Hannah Senesh, translated by Jeff Klepper and Daniel Freelander © 2002.

28 "El malei rachamim," translation from *Mishkan T'filah: A Reform Siddur* © 2007 by the Central Conference of American Rabbis, p. 530.

29 "Shoah Kaddish," by Elie Wiesel, in *The Six Days of Destruction: Meditations toward Hope* © 1988 by Elirion Associates, Central Conference of American Rabbis, and Albert Friedlander, p. 86.

30 "Why did the heavens not darken..." adapted from the Crusade Chronicle of Solomon bar-Simson, in *European Jewry and the First Crusade*, by Robert Hazan, © 1987, by the University of California Press, p. 164.

31 "In the presence of eyes," from "Oath" by Abraham Shlonsky, in *Avraham Shlonsky: Yalkut Shirim*, edited by A. B. Yafeh, Yachdav, Tel Aviv © 1967; translated by Herbert Bronstein, in *Gates of Prayer: The New Union Prayerbook* © 1975, by the Central Conference of American Rabbis, p. 573.

31 "Above a balcony" by Esther Raab, © 2002, Harold Schimmel, appeared first in *Thistles: Selected Poems of Esther Raab*, translated by

Harold Schimmel, published by Ibis Editions, Jersualem, p. 53.

32 "And now Judaism finds," by Ahad Ha'am, in *Nationalism and the Jewish Ethic, Basic Writings of Ahad Ha'am*, edited by Hans Kohn © 1962 by Schocken Books, p. 78.

34 "Are we to ask merely for the right," by Abba Hillel Silver, in *Vision and Victory: A Collection of Addresses, 1942–1948* © 1949 by Zionist Organization of American, p. 20.

35 *Eli Eli (Halichah L'Kesariah)*, by Hannah Senesh © Acum Ltd.

35 "Tzefat," by Danny Siegel, in *Before Our Very Eyes: Readings for a Journey through Israel* © 1986 by The Town House Press, p. 43. Used by permission.

37 "Kinneret," by Rachel Blaustein.

37 "Perhaps," by Rachel Blaustein, translated from Hebrew into Yiddish by Zalman Rubashov-Shazar for the 1931 Yiddish edition of *The Plough Woman: Records of the Pioneer Women in Palestine*, edited and annotated by Mark A. Raider and Miriam B. Raider-Roth; translated into English by Maurice Samuel for the 1932 English edition, copyright © 2002 by University Press of New England, Lebanon, NH. Reprinted with permission, p. 231.

38 "The Kinneret is not simply a landscape," from "On the Shores of the Kinneret" by Rachel Blaustein, originally published in *Shirei Rachel: Sod Kismam*, Sridot: Kiron, 1993, p. 357. Translation by Lisa Katz. Used by permission of Lisa Katz.

38 Ezekiel 47:6–9, *JPS Tanakh* © 1985, 1999 by The Jewish Publication Society, Philadelphia. Reprinted with permission of the University of Nebraska Press.

40 Psalm 121, *JPS Tanakh* © 1985, 1999 by The Jewish Publication Society, Philadelphia. Reprinted with permission of the University of Nebraska Press.

41 Psalm 133:1–3, *JPS Tanakh* © 1985, 1999 by The Jewish Publication Society, Philadelphia. Reprinted with permission of the University of Nebraska Press.

42 "Who are you that come, stepping heavy in silence?" by Yitzhak Lamdan, in *Zionism and the Creation of a New Society*, by Ben Halpern and Jehuda Reinharz © 1998 by Oxford University Press, Inc. p. 151.

43 "After 2,000 Years," by Serge Lippe based on an article by Steven Erlanger, *New York Times*, June 12, 2005.

4. Prayers for Unique Moments in Israel

55 For Israeli Soldiers or Civilians Being Held Captive, composed by
    Rabbi Ofer Sabath Beit-Halachmi, Congregation Tzur-Hadassah, in
    July 2006 when abductors of Israeli soldiers signaled the onset of
    the second Lebanon war. Translated by Rabbi Rachel Sabath Beith-
    Halachmi. Used by permission.

5. Prayers for Specific Occasions

6. Prayers upon Leaving Israel

7. Prayers Upon Returning Home

8. Blessings before and after Eating

9. *Havdalah*

10. Songs of Israel

88 *Shir LaShalom*, text by Moshe Ben-Ari, Globalev World Music Productions Ltd., and Yaakov Rotblit. © Acum Ltd.

Afterword

91 Psalm 137:1–6, *JPS Tanakh* © 1985, 1999 by The Jewish Publication Society, Philadelphia. Reprinted with permission of the University of Nebraska Press.